A YEAR OF BLACK JOY

52 BLACK VOICES SHARE THEIR LIFE PASSIONS

curated by
JAMIA WILSON

illustrated by
JADE ORLANDO

MAGIC CAT PUBLISHING

CONTENTS

JANUARY

8
The Joy of Choreography
Artistic Director **Davalois Fearon**
International Choreographers Day

10
The Joy of Flowers
Florist **Hazel Gardiner**
International Flower Day

12
The Joy of Hugs
Life Coach **David Hale Sylvester**
National Hugging Day

14
The Joy of Learning
Musician **Nathan Holder**
International Day of Education

18
The Joy of Habitats
Conservationist **Tolga Aktas**
World Wetlands Day

20
The Joy of Science
Scientist **Dr. Raven 'the Science Maven' Baxter**
International Day of Women and Girls in Science

22
The Joy of Languages
Linguist **Dr. John McWhorter**
International Mother Language Day

FEBRUARY

16
The Joy of Allyship
Activist and Human Rights Defender **Lady Phyll**
LGBT+ History Month

MARCH

24
The Joy of Story Hunting
Author **Patrice Lawrence**
World Book Day

26
The Joy of Being a Black Woman
Activist **Tabitha St. Bernard-Jacobs**
International Women's Day

28

The Joy of Eating Together
Chef **Amanda Yee**
Spring Equinox

30

The Joy of Poetry
Poet **Lemn Sissay**
World Poetry Day

32

The Joy of
Forecasting the Weather
Meteorologist **Alex Wallace**
World Meteorological Day

APRIL

34

The Joy of Representation
Producer and Storyteller
Laura Henry-Allain
Diversity Month

36

The Joy of Homes
Interior Designer **Michelle Ogundehin**
National Decorating Month

38

The Joy of Murals
Artist **Tatyana Fazlalizadeh**
World Art Day

40

The Joy of Vaccines
Doctor of Emergency Medicine
Dr. Ronx Ikharia
World Immunisation Week

MAY

42

The Joy of
Community Gardening
Gardener **Tayshan Hayden-Smith**
National Gardening Week

44

The Joy of Drawing
Illustrator **Jade Orlando**
National Drawing Day

46

The Joy of Biodiversity
Wildlife TV Presenter **Gillian Burke**
International Day for Biological Diversity

48

The Joy of My Culture
Student **Chantale Zuzi**
World Day for Cultural Diversity for
Dialogue and Development

JUNE

50
The Joy of Tiny Ocean Dwellers
Oceanographer **Dr. Bethanie Edwards**
World Ocean Day

52
The Joy of Bees
Beekeeper **Samantha 'Foxx' Winship**
Summer Equinox

54
The Joy of World Music
Ethnomusicologist **Dr. Birgitta Johnson**
World Music Day

56
The Joy of Being Smart on Social Media
Lifestyle Blogger **Dr. Marie Lahai**
@rie_defined
World Social Media Day

JULY

58
The Joy of Laughter
Comedian **Inel Tomlinson**
International Joke Day

60
The Joy of Entrepreneurship
Entrepreneur **Andy Ayim**
World Youth Skills Day

62
The Joy of Chess
Grandmaster **Maurice Ashley**
World Chess Day

64
The Joy of Creative Self-care
Artist **Andrea Pippins**
International Self-Care Day

AUGUST

66
The Joy of Wheelchair Racing
Athlete **Anne Wafula Strike**
Summer Paralympic Games

68
The Joy of Photography
Photographer and filmmaker
Nganji Mutiri
World Photography Day

70
The Joy of Threads
Broadcaster **Miquita Oliver**
World Fashion Day

72
The Joy of Dogs
House Dogge Founder
Angela Medlin
International Dog Day

SEPTEMBER

74
The Joy of Classical Music
Cellist **Sheku Kanneh-Mason**
Classical Music Month

76
The Joy of Breathing
Breathwork Coach **Kathleen Booker**
Mindfulness Day

78
The Joy of Democracy
Politician **David Lammy**
International Day of Democracy

80
The Joy of Autumn Food
Chef **Andi Oliver**
Autumn Equinox

82
The Joy of Travel
Digital Creator **Phil Calvert**
@philwaukee
World Tourism Day

OCTOBER

84
The Joy of Styling Hair
Celebrity Hairstylist **Yene Damtew**
National Hair Day

86
The Joy of Buildings
Architect **Sade Akinsanya**
World Architecture Day

88
The Joy of Looking Up
Space Scientist
Dr. Maggie Aderin-Pocock
World Space Week

90
The Joy of Birds
Urban Birder **David Lindo**
World Migratory Bird Day

92
The Joy of Fossils
Palaeontologist **Dr. Lisa White**
National Fossil Day

94
The Joy of Archaeology
Archaeologist
Dr. Ayana Flewellen
International Archaeology Day

NOVEMBER

96
The Joy of STEM
Cofounder of Stemettes
Dr. Anne-Marie Imafidon
National STEM Day

98
The Joy of Owning Your Voice
Podcasters **Sandria Washington** and
Dr. Samantha Coleman
World Adoption Day

100
The Joy of Activism
Climate Justice Activist **Vanessa Nakate**
Global Day of Action for Climate Justice

102
The Joy of Rugby
Rugby Football Union Chairman
Tom Ilube
National Rugby Day

106
The Joy of Mountains
Adventurer **Sibusiso Vilane**
International Mountain Day

108
The Joy of Plant History
Plant Historian **Advolly Richmond**
Winter Equinox

110
The Joy of Making
Crafter **Nerrisa Pratt**
Christmas

DECEMBER

104
The Joy of Animals
Zookeeper and Wildlife Educator
Jungle Jordan
World Wildlife Conservation Day

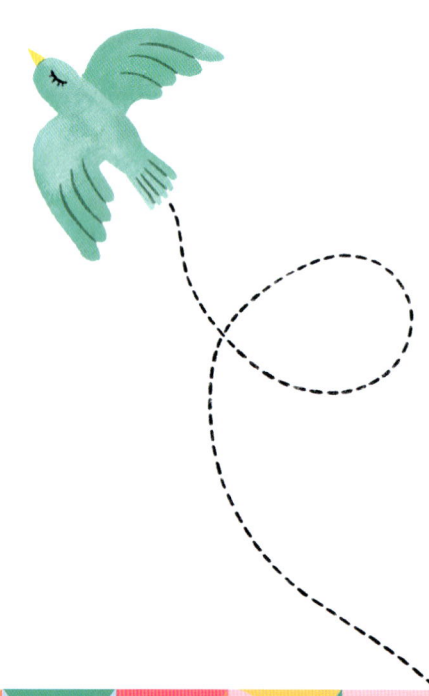

Dear Reader,
What brings you joy?

This is among my favourite questions to ask folks because it almost always brings a smile to their face and, in turn, my own.

One of the biggest joys of my life has been my devotion to books as a reader, editor and author. That's why I'm delighted to invite you to take this journey with us to celebrate joy with a selection of 52 global Black visionaries, creators and changemakers who cover topics from astrology to astronomy, and beekeeping to baking. We welcome you to revel in the glorious diversity of Black life and tap into their joys through new discoveries like seasonal recipes, indoor and outdoor arts and crafts, and much more.

Joy is limitless and can inspire, connect, heal and transform individuals, communities and the world. And Black joy is as diverse as we are as a diaspora of people with myriad cultures, languages, ideas and interests. Through these pages, you're invited to lean into your curiosity and let your imagination allow you to embrace the pleasure and beauty of being who you are and doing what lights up your life.

Joyfully,
Jamia

Activist, author and editor

INTERNATIONAL CHOREOGRAPHERS DAY

THE JOY OF CHOREOGRAPHY

Artistic Director
Davalois Fearon

Dance is life; dance is love; dance is everything. How I feel my body bend, shake and express itself is a unique experience no other art form can provide.

Dance fills me with a sense of belonging and ownership of myself and my life choices. Dance allows me to feel empowered and connected to my ancestral bloodline of the folks who came before me and blessed me with knowledge. When I dance, I am levitated to another place in space and time where I am powerful beyond belief. This power gives me great joy knowing that I am always in full control.

Feeling grounded, abandoning self-judgment and gaining a deep acceptance of myself is a joy that can only be felt through the body. To move your bones, your joints, your muscles and to exert yourself is true living and thus pure joy!

> *When I dance, I am levitated to another place in space and time where I am powerful beyond belief.*

Davalois's Dance Academy

In dance, choreography is the act of inventing steps and movements. One of the true gifts of dance is being able to say something through the dance you design.

A dance can be **SOLO** (which means one person), a **DUET** (which means two people), or a **TRIO** (three people), and so on.

Through choreography, you can show a particular action or feeling in how you **ARRANGE** your dancers.

For example, to show uniqueness, you could show a **COLLECTIVE** of dancers dressed all in green, lifting and supporting the **SOLOIST**, who could be wearing pink.

All of this can be said without a single word — it's all in the **MOVEMENT** and **ARRANGEMENT**.

JANUARY

INTERNATIONAL FLOWER DAY

THE JOY OF FLOWERS

Florist Hazel Gardiner

Flowers are enchanting in their kaleidoscope of colours. There are hundreds of thousands of varieties, and I'm lucky enough to assemble these beautiful blooms.

The best thing about being a florist is that you become an explorer of your surroundings with new, inquisitive eyes. I observe and investigate, look upwards and down low. I may find giant palm leaves, dusky wheat dried by the sun or branches free of leaves, lost by cool temperatures. I use all these botanical gifts in my work, guiding each thoughtfully into place. To me, a fragrant garden rose can be as breathtaking as a humble dandelion growing quietly in the cracks of the pavement.

It's not only what I use, but the physical action of using my hands to create, that transforms my emotions and feelings. Designing with flowers transports me to a joy-filled place, much as you may feel turning the pages of this joyful book.

> *Designing with flowers transports me to a joy-filled place.*

Hazel's Guide to Pressing Flowers

Pressing flowers is a wonderful creative process that encourages you to explore. You'll not only preserve flowers, but also the memories that came with them.

MATERIALS
- Fresh flowers
- Absorbent blotting or tissue paper
- A notebook
- Heavy books
- Tweezers

METHOD

1. Make sure your flowers are completely dry, then remove any unwanted leaves and trim down the stems.

2. Fold a piece of blotting or tissue paper in half. Place your fresh materials face down, on one side, making sure none are touching.

3. Fold the paper over and place it inside a thick notebook. Then repeat, adding your next layer of selections at intervals of 10–15 pages.

4. Place several heavy books on top of your notebook and wait. (It's tempting to check, but don't disturb them for at least two weeks. If they're still moist, replace the blotting or tissue paper and wait another one to two weeks until fully dried.)

5. When they're dry, gently remove your pressed flowers with tweezers.

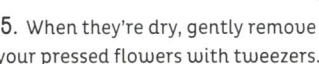

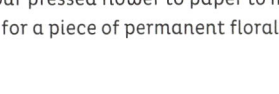

6. It's now time to get artistic! You can attach your pressed flower to paper to make greeting cards for a friend, or place it in a clear locket for a piece of permanent floral jewellery.

JANUARY

NATIONAL HUGGING DAY

THE JOY OF HUGS

Life Coach
David Hale Sylvester

Since 2001, I have travelled through America's 50 states and 42 countries, amassing over half a million hugs.

It all began when the World Trade Centre towers were attacked and fell in New York on 11 September 2001, I sought out the one thing to make me feel better: a hug. It has been the journey of a lifetime and I have had to evolve in every way possible. I have become more approachable, open and honest. A simple hug has been my portal to becoming a better man in many ways.

> There's so much joy to be found in embracing others.

Hugs are essential to a happy life and the best part of who we can be. There's so much joy to be found in embracing others. Start with your family, expand your hug circle to your friends, and then offer a hug to someone you've never hugged before and make the world better — one hug at a time.

JANUARY

David's Guide to Hugging

Hugs are very special and possibly the best part of who we can be, so take particular care and hug someone how you want to be held. Ask someone if they feel comfortable with being hugged and what kind of hugs feel right to them.

SMILE at the person you want to share your love with to make them feel welcome. Smiles are like facial hugs.

Open your arms to signal that you'd like a hug. With your **ARMS OPEN WIDE**, take a few steps towards the person.

Let them take one step towards you. Then **WRAP YOUR ARMS** around them like they are the only person in the world, and hold them close enough to feel safe and secure.

A great hug is a **MINDFUL PRACTICE**. Notice the pressure of their body against yours, and all the thoughts that pop up in your mind. Hold them long enough to feel your warmth, and then let go and say, "Thank you".

And one day, they will return the favour when you need a warm embrace.

INTERNATIONAL DAY OF EDUCATION

THE JOY OF LEARNING

Musician Nathan Holder

My music education didn't start in school. It started at home and at church, watching and listening to incredible musicians.

I've been fortunate to travel around the world because of music — either through playing my saxophone or teaching others about ways we can make music education a more inclusive and diverse experience.

I've always been fascinated with music — not just playing or listening to it, but learning about the people who create it and their stories. People who have overcome great odds, been written out of history or found unique ways to tell their stories through sound. Every time I make a connection with musicians past or present, I feel a rush of energy that surges through my body that inspires me to write, play and ultimately share. Learning about the wonderful world of music can encourage anyone to dive into creation, expression and joy.

> Every time I make a connection with musicians past or present, I feel a rush of energy that surges through my body.

14

JANUARY

Musicians Who Inspire Nathan

These are just some of the musicians who I've learnt about and have made a big impact in my life.

SISTER ROSETTA THARPE
Often called the GODMOTHER OF ROCK 'N' ROLL, Rosetta inspired many well-known Rock 'n' Roll stars of the twentieth century with her powerful vocals and electric guitar playing. She was among the first popular recording artists to use heavy distortion on her electric guitar.

SAMUEL COLERIDGE-TAYLOR
Born in London in 1875, Samuel was an accomplished VIOLINIST and COMPOSER. He wrote music inspired by his West African heritage and fought against racial prejudice with his incredible compositions. His best-known work was Hiawatha's Wedding Feast, which has been performed around the world since its creation.

LORD KITCHENER
After singing a song on the steps of the SS Empire Windrush in 1948, Lord Kitchener, affectionately named Kitch, helped introduce CALYPSO to Britain. He was a trailblazer of his time, and a central figure who helped spread Trinbagonian music around the world.

SHIRLEY J. THOMPSON, OBE
An award-winning COMPOSER, Shirley has written music to commemorate some of the most prominent events in British history over the past twenty years. One of her most well-known pieces was New Nation Rising: A 21st Century Symphony, a composition which was commissioned for the Queen's Golden Jubilee.

LGBT+ HISTORY MONTH

THE JOY OF ALLYSHIP

Activist and Human Rights Defender Lady Phyll

Little Black girls are the best allies in the world. I know this because I was one — and I'm still an ally today, working to support the rights of LGBTQ+ people across the world.

I was a powerful little Black girl. I defended people on the playground; I asked questions in class when things didn't make sense for me and for other people — and because I questioned how the world worked around me, I learned that allyship means to speak up. Little Black girls are the best allies in the world because we pay attention, we use our voices and we won't stand for injustice.

When we rise together, we are mighty. I'm proof that when we stand our ground and use our voices, allies can help people all over the world be free, safe and equal. I'm proud to be an ally to those who need a strong friend, a loud voice and big hug. Little Black girls are the best allies in the world, who become the best Black women in the world. I know this because I am one.

> *When we rise together, we are mighty.*

16

FEBRUARY

Some of the rights LGBTQ+ people have today are thanks to allies of the past. Each of us carries on the legacy, and one day in the future I want someone to say, "I fight for what's right because Phyll helped prepare me and the world for this work", in the same way that I honour our ancestors.

LGBTQ+ stands for lesbian, gay, bi, trans and queer. The + is an inclusive symbol to mean 'and others' to include people of all identities.

MARSHA P. JOHNSON and **SYLVIA RIVERA** were trans women (assigned male at birth but whose gender identity is female) who dedicated their life to allyship.

Both women became prominent figures in the **STONEWALL UPRISINGS**, a series of demonstrations by members of the LGBTQ+ community in New York in 1969.

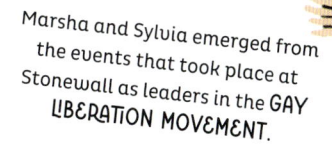

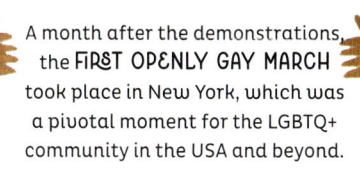

Marsha and Sylvia emerged from the events that took place at Stonewall as leaders in the **GAY LIBERATION MOVEMENT**.

A month after the demonstrations, the **FIRST OPENLY GAY MARCH** took place in New York, which was a pivotal moment for the LGBTQ+ community in the USA and beyond.

Together they also helped found **STAR (STREET TRANSVESTITE ACTION REVOLUTIONARIES)**, a group that supported transgender youth experiencing homelessness.

17

WORLD WETLANDS DAY

THE JOY OF HABITATS

Conservationist Tolga Aktas

Growing up, I travelled back and forth between countries. From the wetlands in the UK to the mountains in Cyprus to the forests in Jamaica, I took joy in discovering various habitats from an early age.

For decades, people passionate about the natural world have been working hard to protect our habitats — and the wildlife that call them home. I am proud to be one of these people; as a conservationist, I believe protecting our natural world will be the most important mission we commit to.

From food to shelter, a good habitat provides everything we could possibly need to survive. There is real hope for our beautiful planet if we put all our energy, time and love towards protecting it. Our actions as a species on Earth can either positively or negatively impact our natural world, and it is up to us to find a balance that works in unity for the greater good.

There is real hope for our beautiful planet.

Tolga's Guide to Wetlands

Wetlands are areas of land that are covered by water — either seasonally or permanently. They come in all shapes and sizes, and take many forms.

RIVERS AND STREAMS are the most familiar wetlands to most of us. We need them for lots of reasons: for **FRESH DRINKING WATER**, to carry nutrients, and in some countries, as community places for bathing and laundry.

ESTUARIES are areas where freshwater rivers or streams meet the salty ocean. They provide safe places for small fish, shellfish and migrating birds. They are often called the **NURSERIES OF THE SEA** because so many species rely on these habitats for nesting and breeding.

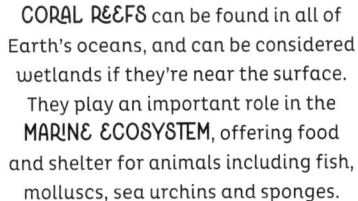

MANGROVES form when trees grow in thick clusters along seashores and riverbanks in the tropics. Their dense roots **BIND AND BUILD SOIL**, which helps form barriers against natural disasters like storms and floods.

CORAL REEFS can be found in all of Earth's oceans, and can be considered wetlands if they're near the surface. They play an important role in the **MARINE ECOSYSTEM**, offering food and shelter for animals including fish, molluscs, sea urchins and sponges.

FEBRUARY

INTERNATIONAL DAY OF WOMEN AND GIRLS IN SCIENCE

THE JOY OF SCIENCE

Scientist Dr. Raven 'the Science Maven' Baxter

I always knew I wanted to be a scientist. When I was a little girl, I conducted experiments with anything I could get my hands on.

Today, I am a molecular biologist — which means I study cells. The best thing about what I do is getting to exchange ideas among my fellow scientists. I love when there is diversity of talent, because when you bring differences to the table, you're automatically expanding the capabilities of the entire group.

Being a scientist means that each day brings new opportunities — we may find something that's new to the entire universe, learn more about a certain topic or validate a scientific theory. Science is at the core of making life better for all living things — whether through medical cures or discoveries that will develop over time into solutions for the world's greatest problems.

> *Science is at the core of making life better for all living things.*

Dr. Raven's First Scientific Success

The first time I conducted an experiment until I was satisfied with the outcome was when I constructed paper aeroplanes at the age of seven.

Using pages from my notebook, I FOLDED paper aeroplanes into different shapes and sizes.

Then, I LAUNCHED them into the air to watch how far they went.

I'd ask myself...
Which aeroplane will travel the FARTHEST distance?
Which aeroplane will spend the LONGEST time in the air?
Which aeroplane will land CLOSEST to a target?

After that, I'd go back and fold them in different ways to achieve the best OUTCOME.

With each new TAKE OFF, I was learning better ways to build my planes, and the higher they flew, the happier I got — and the better scientist I became.

INTERNATIONAL MOTHER LANGUAGE DAY

THE JOY OF LANGUAGES

Linguist
Dr. John McWhorter

I remember the first time I heard another language.

I was born and raised in Philadelphia in the 1960s, and had a sheltered upbringing. For the first few years of my life, I only ever heard American English. I was five years old when I heard another language for the first time: Hebrew. I was stunned and, quite honestly, I felt left out. I wanted to know the code; I wanted to be able to join in. That moment was when my love of languages was born.

Learning a new language became my version of completing a jigsaw or crossword puzzle. What is it about gaining a new language that I so love? Ironically, words escape me. But I know how it makes me feel: happy. The real magic of language is that it helps me connect with other people. There's nothing much more joyful than that!

> The real magic of language is that it helps me connect with other people.

Language Q&A with Dr. John

Our spoken language not only defines us humans as a species, but it also charms us with its endless mysteries.

HOW DID DIFFERENT LANGUAGES COME TO BE?

Linguists have long struggled to pinpoint a moment of when languages formed. Some people believe that all languages ever spoken **ORIGINATED FROM ONE SINGLE LANGUAGE** that spread across the world; other people believe that languages **EVOLVED AT THE SAME TIME** in different parts of the world.

WHY DON'T WE ALL SPEAK THE SAME LANGUAGE?

There are two reasons: the first is that our world has so much diversity that, when moving from one area to another, the **LANGUAGE CHANGES**. The second is that **LANGUAGE IS IDENTITY**. People communicate more than ideas; they share who they are, what they believe and where they're from.

WHY DOES LANGUAGE CHANGE OVER TIME?

As time passes, **NEW WORDS ARE INVENTED** to describe things that didn't exist before. And sometimes old words get new meanings. A good example of this is the word 'Nice': Over 700 years, it has changed its meaning from 'foolish' to 'dainty' to 'delightful', to today's meaning of 'giving satisfaction'.

HOW DOES A LANGUAGE BECOME EXTINCT?

Some languages become extinct quickly when small communities of speakers are hit by tragedies like natural disasters or wars. Most languages, though, die out gradually as successive generations of speakers become **BILINGUAL** (fluent in two or more languages) and then begin to lose proficiency in their traditional language.

FEBRUARY

WORLD BOOK DAY

THE JOY OF STORY HUNTING

Author Patrice Lawrence

The world is full of stories waiting for me to discover and write down. Stories are calling out to me from behind bushes, through the windows of tall buildings and in the ebb and flow of rivers.

○★⋯⋯⋯○★○

I love asking strange questions and starting to write.

○★⋯⋯⋯○★○

I was that child who was always asking questions. Now that I'm an adult, those questions are the tools I use for my story hunt.

What if I peek behind that bush and find that there's a world ruled by warrior worms? What are their secret plans?

Why does a sad monster lurk behind that tower window? Perhaps she's locked in, missing her family and trying to make a parachute out of the paper left in the office. (But where is everybody else and how did she get there?)

Why does the river have waves like the sea? What if there are rivermen deep below, weaving the water on giant looms? What would happen if they stopped?

I love asking strange questions, gathering my even stranger answers, picking up a pen and starting to write…

MARCH

Patrice's Questions to Find Your Story

When writing a book, I ask myself the questions below to help me work out what's going to happen. Perhaps you can do the same when you're writing your stories. Good luck!

WHO is my main character?	WHO are their friends and family?	DO they have any enemies? Why?
WHAT is precious to my character?	WHAT are they afraid of?	WHAT do they want?
WHO or what is stopping them from getting what they want?	WHAT is their life usually like?	WHAT changes to kick-start the story?
WHAT is the first challenge my character faces to stop them from getting what they want?	HOW do they overcome it?	WHAT makes my character nearly give up?
WHAT makes them pull through?	WHAT do they get at the end of the story?	WHAT do they learn?

INTERNATIONAL WOMEN'S DAY

THE JOY OF BEING A BLACK WOMAN

Activist Tabitha St. Bernard-Jacobs

I am a Black woman. I am an immigrant Black woman. I am a multiracial immigrant Black woman. I am all these things at once.

I moved to the United States as a teenager from Trinidad & Tobago. In T&T, I was in the racial majority. In New York, I went through an American awakening of sorts, discovering what my identity meant in a place where Black womanhood is often silenced and disregarded. As I came into my own, I realized my Blackness is a part of my soul and my joy holds roots in my ancestors' gifts.

My Blackness is a part of my soul.

As one of the organizers of the Women's March movement, I have spent a great deal of time fighting for gender equity — and it is Black joy that replenishes me when the effects of gender injustice and racism become too much. It is in the pride that bounces off my melanin, dances along with the coils of my curls and the round of my nose. It is my joy.

Tabitha's Manifesto for Expansive Soul Care

I centre my love for myself around a practice of expansive soul care, inspired by psychotherapist Sarah Harris. Black women deserve joy like everyone else. Here are just some of the ways I practice expansive soul care.

JOURNALLING
Putting pen to paper allows me to get my thoughts and feelings out of my head and be present in the moment. Every day I try to write things I am grateful for, centered around my relationship with myself and my body.

MARCH

GETTING INTO NATURE
Mother Earth grounds me while sending sweet reminders that I am in a relationship with all it has to offer. Going out into nature helps me breathe, relax and centre myself.

WEARING NATURAL HAIR
Natural hair gives me freedom. My afro helps me feel empowered and confident in my own skin. It's the natural crown that I've been chosen to carry and I do so with joy.

HARNESSING POWER
The Women's March movement is pivotal to my work. Our mission is to harness the political power of everyday women to create transformative social change. Protests are a direct expression of expansive soul care because I'm fighting for the world my children and I deserve.

CELEBRATING BLACK WOMEN
What joy it is to celebrate life, love and vibrancy through the Black women who impact my life. I imagine that I help nurture their expansive soul care when I reflect the love they give to me.

SPRING EQUINOX

THE JOY OF EATING TOGETHER

Chef Amanda Yee

When most people think of joy, they think of a happy feeling. For me, I think of joy as a verb. Joy is something we choose to consciously practise. One of the ways I practise joy is by eating food with my loved ones.

> Spring is the perfect time to eat together.

Spring is the perfect time to eat together because of what spring represents. Spring is Mother Nature's way of promising us that there is hope. The sun shines. Animals come out of hibernation. Flowers bloom. And some of the best foods are ready to eat!

I love seeing the smiles on people's faces when they take their first bite of food. I love hearing them laugh over a good joke. To create room for people to enjoy themselves, we make the space comfortable for others: we set the table, we cut flowers, we prepare the season's best produce and we get out the good plates.

Amanda's Tips for Entertaining

Food, drink, friends, good conversation — a party is a combination of ingredients. Throwing one takes time and effort, but it's also so much fun.

Pick a **DATE** and **TIME** to host your party. Will there be a theme? What about a dress code?

Write a list of all the **PEOPLE** you want to invite. Friends from school? Family members?

Pick a **PLACE** where you will host your party. Is it in your home? In your garden? Does it have an area to prepare all the food?

Create a **MENU**. Sometimes I make something I really love to eat, or sometimes I pick things that I think people will love to eat.

Make or buy any **DECORATIONS**, and create a playlist of your favourite music to listen to.

Send out **INVITES**. Include the event's date, time and occasion in the invite. If you're asking people to bring stuff, include this in the invite.

Review your **RECIPES** and see how much time you need to prepare. I like to do as much as I can before the party starts, so I can spend more time with my guests on the day.

And when the day arrives, have **FUN!**

MARCH

29

WORLD POETRY DAY

THE JOY OF POETRY

Poet Lemn Sissay

When I write a poem, I capture a memory that I can revisit any time. If I want to recall a wonderful holiday, a beautiful sunrise or a good friend, then I write a poem and take that writing with me wherever I go. Before long, I have a book of memories.

> When I write a poem, I capture a memory that I can revisit any time.

When I was a boy, I didn't live with my birth parents; I lived in children's homes and foster care. I moved from place to place. I moved from family to family. And I could remember all these places and people by writing poems.

I soon realized I could discover a whole new world from my imagination through poetry. I could visit it, too. I could discover wonderful things, places I could call home. So, I will tell you a secret. A special secret. My home is *here* in these words. And by reading them, you have opened the front door. Welcome! Come on in!

Everything Is Still by Lemn Sissay

In this poem, I'm revisiting my childhood, when all was well. Everything changed for me shortly after, so this poem is a way of remembering how good things were for a brief time.

The cat curled cautiously in a corner
And the dog dozed on the doormat.
The pets slept as the maid swept
The clock clicked and toc ticked
All the dot-to-dots have been done
And all the colouring in has been filled
And all the games played are won
And everything is still.

As if the looming moon itself did cry
Snow slipped from the sloping sky
And limboed under the lamplight
A flock of white butterflies by night
They weave their way through wind
And rest upon home and hill
And melt into everything
'Til everything is still.

The darling buds of day are done
The leaping loop of light is run
Now sleeps the blue sky and its sun
With nothing lost and nothing won
The mist lies upon the quiet crops
And the wind sleeps on the windowsill
And the moon rests on the rooftops
And everything is still…

WORLD METEOROLOGICAL DAY

THE JOY OF FORECASTING THE WEATHER

Meteorologist Alex Wallace

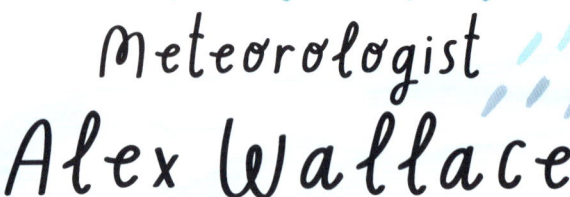

Weather is all around us. No matter where you live or the colour of your skin, the weather affects every living being on this planet.

So much of what we do in life relies on the weather. You may wonder if your PE class will be moved inside because of the rain, or if school is cancelled after a storm.

As a child, I was curious about the science behind the weather and its impact on people. That is one of the reasons why I chose to become a weatherperson, also known as a meteorologist.

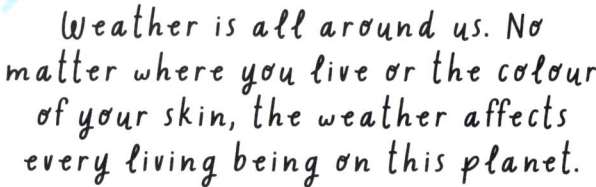

It makes my day to help you plan yours.

Meteorologists can use tools to predict the weather. We don't always get it right. Sometimes Mother Nature is unpredictable. Although, I think our average is pretty good, and it makes my day to help you plan your day.

Alex's Weather Forecasting Tools

If you look out your window, you might think you can tell what the weather is. But we need lots of data to predict the weather, and this information comes from different weather tools.

We use a **THERMOMETER** to measure how hot or cold the air is. Weather thermometers are kept in a Stevenson screen, which is a white box with slats that allow air to flow through.

An **ANEMOMETER** is used to measure wind. It's an important tool, as wind transports moisture and temperature from one area to another. Therefore weather conditions change with the shift of wind direction.

WEATHER SATELLITES float around in space and orbit Earth. These satellites have sensors that scan Earth and monitor its ever-changing weather and climate.

BAROMETERS measure air pressure, which is the force caused by the weight of the air above us in the atmosphere. Generally, a rising barometer means dry conditions are on the way, and a falling barometer means rain is on its way.

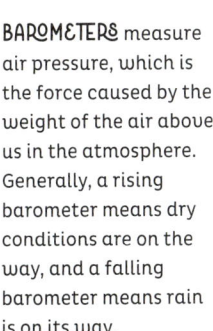

WEATHER BALLOONS float up into the atmosphere, carrying instruments that gather information on temperature, humidity (the amount of water vapour in the air), atmospheric pressure and wind speed.

MARCH

33

DIVERSITY MONTH

THE JOY OF REPRESENTATION

Producer and Storyteller Laura Henry-Allain

I love telling and sharing stories. Whether it is by talking to people, writing books or creating children's television shows, my stories are full of happiness.

It is important to me to show a wide range of characters from different places and cultures, and show people celebrating the unique joys in their lives. My storytelling sometimes mirrors my childhood, such as *JoJo & Gran Gran*, which was based on my relationship with my grandmother, Marie Helena. She lived to 101 and radiated joy!

I want all readers and listeners to feel the joy radiate from characters who look and act like them.

I want all readers and listeners to feel the joy radiate from characters who look and act like them. Joy comes as a gift when you least expect it, and it's the sign of a beautiful life. My purpose in creating this joy is to make others joyful.

Laura's 'Representation' Poem

THE FIRST TIME I SAW ME REPRESENTED IN A STORY...

"Wait a minute," I said to myself.

They have the same skin colour as me!

They have the same lips as me!

They have the same hair as me!

They have the same nose as me!

The food was the same!

I saw my family!

I heard the same voices!

You know what?

I was filled with joy!

THE FIRST TIME I SAW YOU REPRESENTED IN A STORY...

Sharing your joy,

I smiled and was filled with joy and happiness.

How wonderful that I can see and hear that we share so many similar things.

I loved learning that we have differences.
I learned so much from everything that brings you joy.

Most of all, our joys are unique, and our joys are in our hearts.

NATIONAL DECORATING MONTH

THE JOY OF HOMES

Interior Designer
Michelle Ogundehin

When we surround ourselves with things that we love, it can make us feel happy, safe and protected. A warm, fuzzy feeling can come from how we decorate our homes.

It's about pinning up favourite posters. It's being able to dress our bed with colourful pillows. And this is something our ancestors have been doing since the beginning of time. Maybe not hanging posters or adding pillows exactly, but certainly decorating their caves with pictures representing their lives. It was a way of claiming ownership of their space, and it also celebrated who they were as people.

I want to make a space feel like my own unique little corner of the world.

Today we might be more sophisticated in the ways we decorate, but the goal is the same: making a space feel like our own unique little corner of the world, which helps us feel like we really belong in this world, too.

Michelle's Happy Home Advice

Your home is important to how you feel!
Here are four ways to inject some joy at home:

CLEAR THE CLUTTER
If you feel stressed, the last thing you need to see is clutter all around you — yet the two things often go hand in hand. So a **CLEAR OUT** can be incredibly therapeutic! Plus, all your unwanted things could be someone else's treasures.

ADD SOME COLOUR
A few brightly coloured cushions and lamps can transform a whole room. It's the same if you're able to paint even one small wall. Colour is **ENERGIZING** and adds joy to any space.

CLEAN YOUR WINDOWS
NATURAL LIGHT is nature's free happiness maker! So make sure you're not blocking it out with dirty windows or fussy curtains. Pull blinds up as soon as you wake up and let the daylight work its mood-boosting magic.

INTRODUCE PLANTS
If you don't have a garden, bring greenery inside with a houseplant. The power of nature to calm the mind has been shown in many scientific studies. The colour green is naturally soothing. Plus, plants are like **AIR-CLEANING WIZARDS**!

APRIL

WORLD ART DAY

THE JOY OF MURALS
Artist Tatyana Fazlalizadeh

I've been creating impactful murals since I was in high school. But before me, people have been drawing and painting on walls for thousands of years.

Ancient Egypt and India were some of the first places to see marks made on walls. Imagery depicted the lives of the human beings that lived there. We later began to call those images murals. Contemporary mural-making was largely introduced into modern art by artists like Diego Rivera during the Mexican Muralism movement, which began in the 1920s, followed much later by graffiti art across major cities made by young Black and Brown folks.

Artists tell stories of their lives and circumstances through the act of marking on walls. And like the artists who came before me, I use outdoor walls as canvases to reflect other people's stories and experiences.

I use outdoor walls as canvases to reflect other people's stories and experiences.

And at the same time, I create a system that allows people to tell their own stories and provides them power in that process. It doesn't get much more joyful than that.

Tatyana's Mural-Making Process

I approach mural-making by considering how certain groups, particularly Black folks and women, experience the public space. To achieve this, my process of creating murals begins before I even approach an outdoor wall.

1. I begin by **TALKING** with individuals about who they are and what they want to say to the public.

I always get **PERMISSION** before working on a mural!

2. I then **PHOTOGRAPH** them as a way of recording their lives as they live.

I'm generally a quiet person, but creating murals and engaging with communities is a way for me to practise **USING MY VOICE** in a public way.

3. Lastly, I begin the work of creating a **MURAL** of them from pencil drawings.

I'm also able to provide **ACCESS** to art that goes beyond the indoor walls of museums or galleries.

By painting the faces and words of Black people, women and queer people on outdoor walls, I'm providing **SAFE SPACES** for us to be seen and heard.

APRIL

WORLD IMMUNISATION WEEK

THE JOY OF VACCINES

Doctor of Emergency Medicine
Dr. Ronx Ikharia

The world before vaccines was a scary place. Danger could be found in the foods people ate, the water they drank and the people they touched. But through the brilliance of science, we now have vaccines to protect us.

The recent Covid-19 pandemic was the first time that many of us realized how important vaccines are — and creating a vaccine in under a year was no small feat! I had the privilege of learning how to draw up and administer these vaccines in a vaccination centre in my home town of Hackney in London, and I felt immense pride and joy as I saw my community protected.

It's incredible to think that we have the potential to cure every disease and illness. New science is developing constantly; we have the resources around us on this earth, we just haven't discovered all the answers, but the answers *are* there... and the future is infinite!

> It's incredible to think that we have the potential to cure every disease and illness.

Doctor Ronx's Vaccine Lesson

In 1796, an English doctor called Edward Jenner injected small amounts of a cowpox virus into a patient to protect him from the smallpox virus. This was how the first-ever vaccine was created! You may be wondering why it worked...

1. Your **IMMUNE SYSTEM** helps fight off infection from harmful bacteria or viruses by creating antibodies. Each **ANTIBODY** is specific to the bacteria or virus that has entered your body and triggers a specific immune response.

2. These antibodies stay in your immune system after the **INFECTION** has gone, so if you have the same disease again, your immune system remembers and destroys the disease.

3. However, sometimes your immune system isn't always strong enough against the harmful bacteria or virus, and you can become **UNWELL**.

Enter **VACCINES**! A vaccine contains a harmless form of a specific bacteria or virus that causes the disease you are being protected against.

4. The disease-causing **BACTERIA** or **VIRUS** is broken down into harmless, tiny parts before being used in the vaccine, so that they can trigger an immune response without making you sick.

5. Your immune system **ATTACKS** the harmless bacteria or virus from the vaccine and then produces antibodies against it.

6. Your immune system remembers the disease, so once **VACCINATED**, if you get the disease again, your immune system protects you from getting seriously unwell. How cool!

APRIL

NATIONAL GARDENING WEEK

THE JOY OF COMMUNITY GARDENING

Gardener Tayshan Hayden-Smith

Have you ever spent time in a garden and felt a rush of joy?

It is often our connection to nature that reminds us of our most beautiful memories. Being a gardener was the last thing on my mind growing up. My passion for gardening came at a time when I was struggling after West London's Grenfell Tower Fire in 2017, and I wanted to bring my community closer.

The garden acted as an amazing catalyst to getting my community together. Engaging with our natural surroundings gave us peace of mind. Not only did it lift our spirits, but by tending to our community garden, we in turn offered animals a safe space to create a thriving ecosystem, which our garden relied on to sustain itself. More nature meant happier wildlife — which meant a happier garden and community!

> *The garden acted as an amazing catalyst to getting my community together.*

Tayshan's Guide to Community Gardening

Community gardens can offer you the opportunity to get together with your neighbours to grow your own food, flowers and plants.

TEACH EACH OTHER
You could ask an adult to run weekly gardening classes, sharing how to grow fresh fruit, or trees, from seeds.

CREATE A HAVEN FOR ANIMALS
You could make a compost heap from grass cuttings or vegetable peelings to provide the perfect place for wildlife to live.

PLANT A GIVING GARDEN
Also known as a grow-a-row, plant a giving garden to grow food for people who are hungry in your community.

LISTEN TO EVERY IDEA
One idea leads to another... like using a raised bed for a **SANDBOX**, so very young children can pretend to plant!

MAY

43

NATIONAL DRAWING DAY

THE JOY OF DRAWING

Illustrator Jade Orlando

> At the age of six, I told my parents I wanted to draw the characters on the front of cereal boxes. Back then, I didn't know there was a name for that job: illustration!

Drawing has been my passion since I was old enough to hold a crayon. I'd doodle all over my homework and bring characters to life with my coloured pencils. For me, drawing is my second language. When I don't know what to say in words, I can speak loud and clear with pictures. With colour and shape, I can share my joy.

Drawing is my second language.

Illustration is all around us. From the artwork on greeting cards, to the paintings in this very book! We can even use art to solve problems. We decorate wrapping paper, draw characters for shows and books, and even support social causes with our art. The next time you're out, look around. What illustrations speak to you?

Jade's Step-by-Step Drawing Lessons

From rabbits to robots, monsters to mice, I can recall so many cereal box characters from my childhood. It's easy to draw them, too, if we follow four simple steps.

HOW TO DRAW A CAT

1. Draw a head and a body...

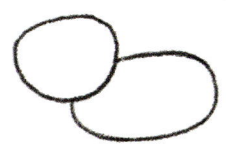

2. add two ears and a fluffy tail...

3. four legs and some whiskers...

4. a face and lots of stripes!

IT'S A CAT!

HOW TO DRAW A ROBOT

1. Draw a body...

2. add two arms and two legs...

3. a head with eyes and an antenna...

4. and its belly screen!

IT'S A ROBOT!

HOW TO DRAW A MONSTER

1. Draw a head...

2. add a long mouth with four teeth...

3. two horns and three eyes...

4. four legs and two arms!

IT'S A MONSTER!

MAY

INTERNATIONAL DAY FOR BIOLOGICAL DIVERSITY

THE JOY OF BIODIVERISTY

Wildlife TV Presenter Gillian Burke

When I was young, I had no idea what the term 'biodiversity' meant, but I would often say, "When I grow up, I want to help make the world a better place for all life".

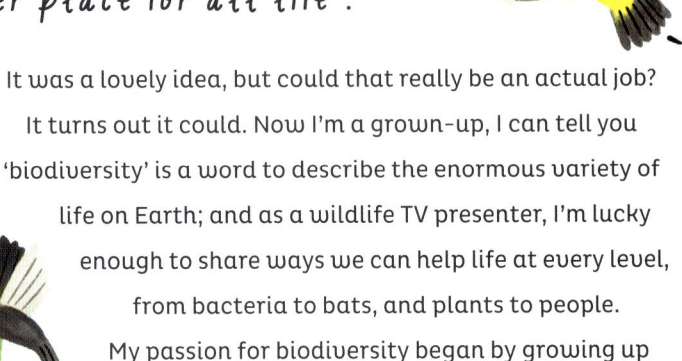

It was a lovely idea, but could that really be an actual job? It turns out it could. Now I'm a grown-up, I can tell you 'biodiversity' is a word to describe the enormous variety of life on Earth; and as a wildlife TV presenter, I'm lucky enough to share ways we can help life at every level, from bacteria to bats, and plants to people. My passion for biodiversity began by growing up in Kenya, where I was always outdoors. I would spend hours crouched under the cover of a hibiscus shrub watching jewel-coloured sunbirds flitting between the bright-red flowers to sip on their nectar. Today, I worry a lot about the state of the planet, and it's easy to end up noticing more of what is wrong and less of what is right. But Mother Earth is always ready to offer up glorious gifts... if you take the time to notice them.

> Mother Earth is always ready to offer up glorious gifts.

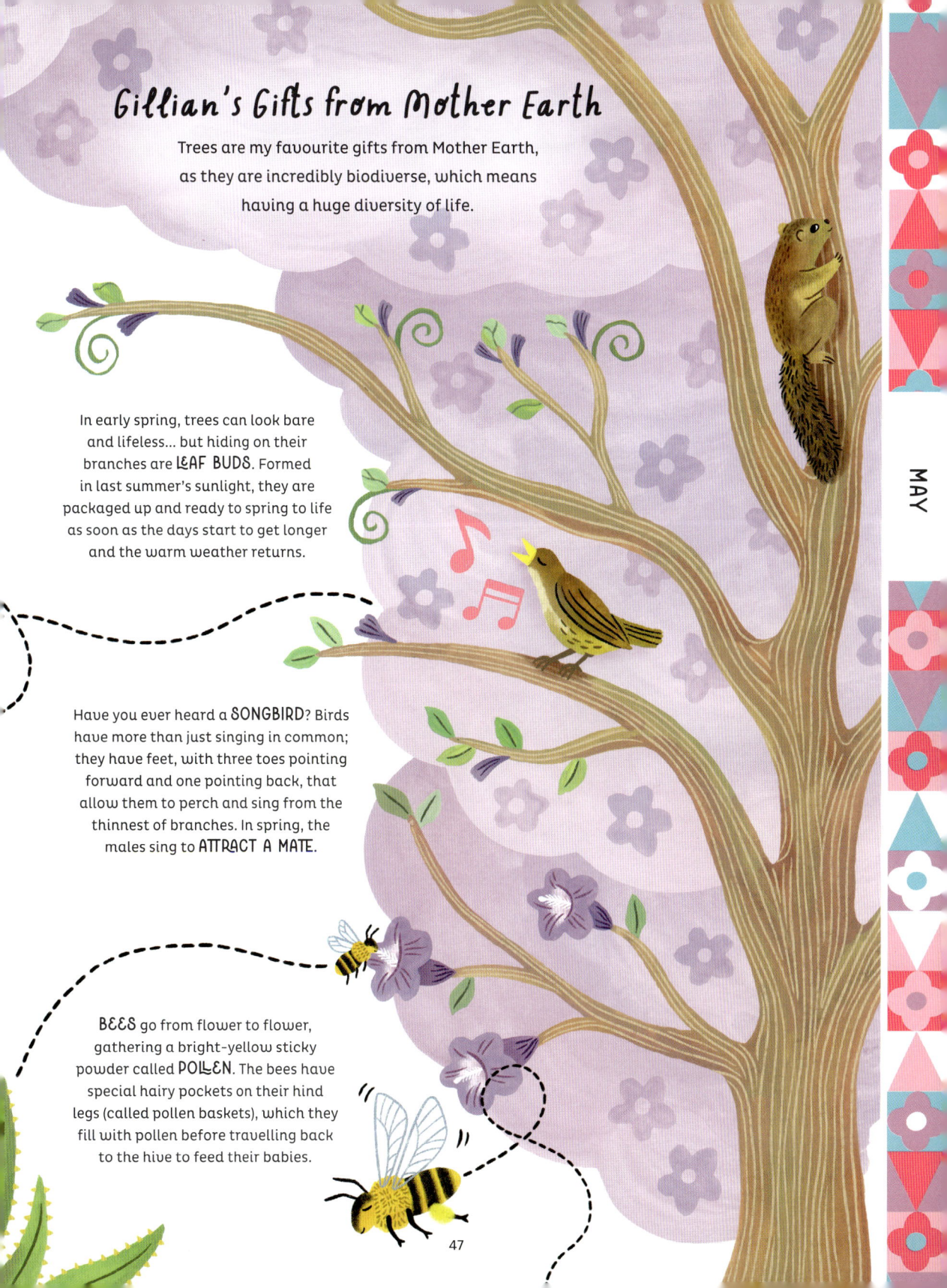

Gillian's Gifts from Mother Earth

Trees are my favourite gifts from Mother Earth, as they are incredibly biodiverse, which means having a huge diversity of life.

In early spring, trees can look bare and lifeless... but hiding on their branches are LEAF BUDS. Formed in last summer's sunlight, they are packaged up and ready to spring to life as soon as the days start to get longer and the warm weather returns.

Have you ever heard a SONGBIRD? Birds have more than just singing in common; they have feet, with three toes pointing forward and one pointing back, that allow them to perch and sing from the thinnest of branches. In spring, the males sing to ATTRACT A MATE.

BEES go from flower to flower, gathering a bright-yellow sticky powder called POLLEN. The bees have special hairy pockets on their hind legs (called pollen baskets), which they fill with pollen before travelling back to the hive to feed their babies.

MAY

WORLD DAY FOR CULTURAL DIVERSITY FOR DIALOGUE AND DEVELOPMENT

THE JOY OF MY CULTURE

Student Chantale Zuzi

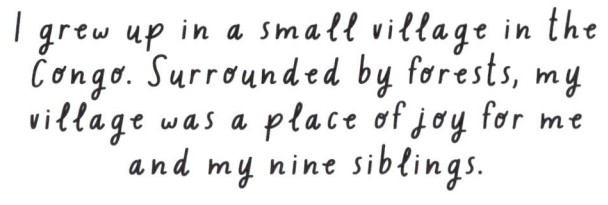

I grew up in a small village in the Congo. Surrounded by forests, my village was a place of joy for me and my nine siblings.

There were pleasures and comforts: familiar smells coming from the outdoor clay kitchens; the scent of the first drops of rain hitting the dusty streets at the end of the dry season; the sounds of drumming and singing; and the sight of our friends and neighbours dancing together.

Sadly, my village was not spared from the wars that ravaged the Congo. Loss swept over us, displacing me and my brothers and sisters, along with thousands of others. But none of the hardships that followed erased my loving attachment to the culture of my childhood. It brings me endless comfort and sustains me today as I navigate a totally different world as a student in the United States.

> *The culture of my childhood brings me endless comfort.*

Chantale's Memories of the Congo Culture

These are some of my deepest impressions from my early years. They are more than memories, though; they are part of who I am, woven into my being, like the colourful threads woven through a length of kitenge cloth.

The handwoven **KITENGE CLOTH** reflects many centuries of our art and craft.

The elaborately constructed **HAIRDOS**, using braids and extensions, are considered essential to the beauty of a woman.

The skills of craftmakers and their textiles, statues, masks and other works are symbols of our rich **ARTISAN CULTURE**.

The history-rich **STORIES** told by ancestors, connecting us with the past and bringing it to life.

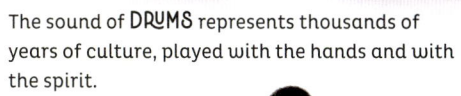

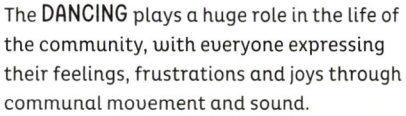

The sound of **DRUMS** represents thousands of years of culture, played with the hands and with the spirit.

The **DANCING** plays a huge role in the life of the community, with everyone expressing their feelings, frustrations and joys through communal movement and sound.

MAY

WORLD OCEAN DAY

THE JOY OF TINY OCEAN DWELLERS

Oceanographer Dr. Bethanie Edwards

Did you know that for the first billion years or so, Earth didn't have breathable oxygen? It wasn't until a type of phytoplankton called cyanobacteria evolved to photosynthesize that the planet was oxygenated.

It fascinated me that these marine bacteria, way too small to see, could have such a massive impact. So I have dedicated my career as an oceanographer to studying the microorganisms that help produce and sustain all life on Earth. These tiny ocean dwellers inspire me to never underestimate myself or the impact of dedicated individuals.

Tiny ocean dwellers inspire me to never underestimate myself.

Phytoplankton's impact is so significant because they contain chlorophyll, which harnesses the sun's energy and converts it into oxygen. It blew my mind when I learned that phytoplankton — who aren't even strong enough to swim against ocean currents — generate as much oxygen for the world as all the trees, shrubs and grasses combined! They also absorb half of the atmosphere's carbon dioxide, which has a positive impact on climate change. How brilliant is that?

Dr. Bethanie's Aquatic Food Web

Along with helping humans and the planet, phytoplankton form the base of the aquatic food web. An aquatic food web is made of interconnected food chains, which show the network of feeding relationships that exists in the ocean.

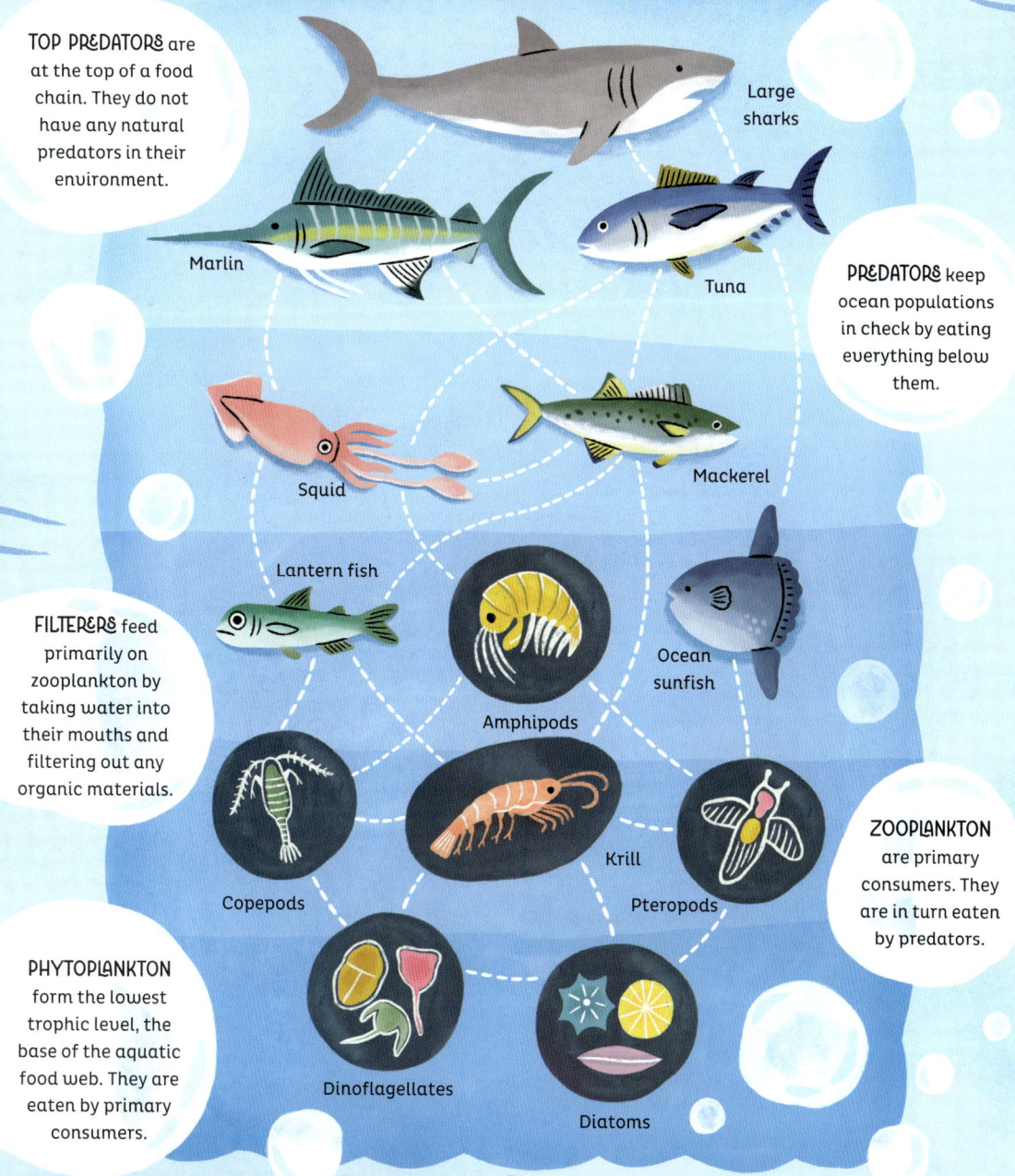

TOP PREDATORS are at the top of a food chain. They do not have any natural predators in their environment.

Large sharks

Marlin

Tuna

PREDATORS keep ocean populations in check by eating everything below them.

Squid

Mackerel

Lantern fish

FILTERERS feed primarily on zooplankton by taking water into their mouths and filtering out any organic materials.

Amphipods

Ocean sunfish

Copepods

Krill

Pteropods

ZOOPLANKTON are primary consumers. They are in turn eaten by predators.

PHYTOPLANKTON form the lowest trophic level, the base of the aquatic food web. They are eaten by primary consumers.

Dinoflagellates

Diatoms

JUNE

SUMMER EQUINOX

THE JOY OF BEES

Beekeeper Samantha 'Foxx' Winship

Nothing could have prepared me for how I'd feel opening a hive for the first time.

I saw a lacework of bees hanging together, leg-to-leg, in a kind of chain. They were using their bodies as scaffolding, working together to build honeycomb. A tear rolled down my cheek as I watched the most beautiful performance I'd ever seen.

This behaviour, known as festooning, inspired me to start my own urban farm in Winston-Salem, North Carolina. On my farm, I manage beehives which produce honey for humans and provide pollination for plants. I also educate visitors on the important role bees play in maintaining our planet. One of every three bites of food we eat depends on bees, and I feel empowered to be able to share that with others. There's truly not a more joyful lesson than learning how to feed yourself and looking after the land and your community.

One of every three bites of food we eat depends on bees.

Samantha's Bee Hotel

I provide a home for bees in the form of a beehive. You can give bees a home, too, in the form of a bee hotel. By doing so, you'll encourage nature in your outside space and help bee populations thrive.

Some bees don't live in hives and instead nest on their own, laying their eggs in tunnels such as in dead wood. A bee hotel copies these conditions to provide a safe place where bees can nest.

MATERIALS
- Hollow stems, such as bramble, reed or bamboo
- Secateurs, or scissors
- A plant pot

METHOD

1. Using one of your stems, **MEASURE** from the bottom of the pot to one centimetre below the rim.

2. With the help of an adult, **CUT EACH STEM** to this length.

3. Carefully **FILL YOUR POT WITH STEMS** until it is tightly packed, making sure the hollow openings face outwards so that bees can get in.

4. Place the pot in a **SUNNY SPOT** that is **SHELTERED** from rain.

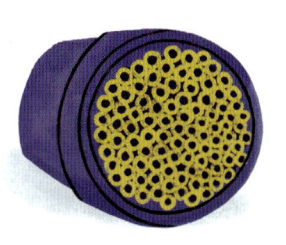

5. Now it's **TIME TO WAIT!** It won't be long until your first guest arrives.

JUNE

WORLD MUSIC DAY

THE JOY OF WORLD MUSIC

Ethnomusicologist Dr. Birgitta Johnson

I love music because music is one of the most universal ways we express ourselves. It entertains us. It inspires us. It is at the centre of what it means to be human.

As an ethnomusicologist, I learn about people's histories, beliefs, traditions and how they think about the world around them through music. I love to play instruments, too, from the Ghanaian instruments like the apentemma to the Afro-Cuban percussion instruments like the batá drums.

As a professor, I have the privilege of teaching courses about music in different cultures around the world, popular music artists like Beyoncé and dance music traditions like rhythm and blues. Music is, after all, a big part of the human experience, no matter where you go in the world.

> Music is a big part of the human experience, no matter where you go in the world.

A Day in the Life of Dr. Birgitta

As an ethnomusicologist, I study music and culture and how they interact in societies worldwide. But you may be wondering what I do all day. Well...

I **LISTEN** to lots of music! I learn about how people express themselves through music and what music means to them and their communities. I study music by reading books and listening to recordings in archives and libraries.

I conduct **FIELDWORK** in communities to learn about music directly from the people who perform, listen to and enjoy it. I speak to everyone from musicians to audience members, composers to radio DJs, and even artists related to music, such as dancers, poets and instrument makers.

I learn how to **PERFORM** music from the musicians and singers in those cultures. I once learned about Afro-Cuban folk music by taking drumming classes from Cuban master percussionist Francisco Aguabella from Matanzas, Cuba.

I **SHARE** what I learn about music in different cultures and social contexts by writing books and articles, producing films and podcasts, participating in documentaries, working for museums and archives, teaching music classes and giving community talks.

JUNE

WORLD SOCIAL MEDIA DAY

THE JOY OF BEING SMART ON SOCIAL MEDIA

Lifestyle Blogger Dr. Marie Lahai @rie_defined

I love to take photos and capture videos of precious moments. From my wedding day to my daughter's first birthday, it brings me and my family so much joy to look back on these milestones.

Never in a million years did I think that my passion for capturing these moments could turn into a career. It surprises people to know that I'm quite shy, and at first I was worried about what people would think of me. But sharing my life online has been such a joyful journey. My photos and videos heal people across the world; they send me messages of the joy that my family's content brings them.

> Sharing my life online has been such a joyful journey.

I spend a lot of time on social media, so it's important to remind myself not to get hooked on likes or compare my life to someone else's. We all have something great to offer the world, and by staying safe online, I can connect with some amazing people who bring me joy. It truly has been one of the biggest blessings of my life!

Dr. Marie's 'SMART' Social Media Tips

Social media can affect how we feel about ourselves and others. These are my 'SMART' tips to make sure I have a healthy relationship with social media.

Start a conversation with myself
I CHECK IN regularly to make sure I'm sharing content that feels good to me. I ask questions like:
- What's the purpose of posting this photo?
- What is it about getting 'likes' that feels good?
- Is looking at social media affecting my mood?

Make sure to stay safe online
I explore the SAFETY AND PRIVACY SETTINGS on my apps. Each one has slightly different settings, but most have the option to set an account to private, or to keep your location hidden.

Avoid too much screen time
I watch out for signs that I am spending too much time on social media, like when I feel anxious when I am separated from my phone. That's when I know it's time to SPEND TIME OFFLINE with my family.

Remember it's carefully curated
Lots of bloggers share 'perfect' content, and that can make you feel pressured to conform to the 'ideal' body or lifestyle. Remember that what people post online is a CURATED VERSION of their life and doesn't always reflect reality.

Try to be kind to myself
It's easy to become focused on how many likes or comments your posts get, which can leave you feeling that you aren't as popular as someone else. I remind myself MY social media is for ME to enjoy, so I post what makes ME feel good.

JUNE

INTERNATIONAL JOKE DAY

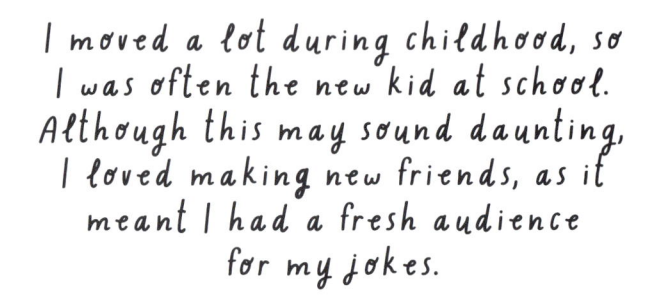

THE JOY OF LAUGHTER

Comedian Inel Tomlinson

I moved a lot during childhood, so I was often the new kid at school. Although this may sound daunting, I loved making new friends, as it meant I had a fresh audience for my jokes.

Making people laugh is one of the greatest feelings in the world. When we laugh, we lighten up; we feel more positive and confident, more hopeful and engaged.

One of the great things about laughter is that it can be crafted in many ways. From telling a knock-knock joke on the playground to doing stand-up comedy on stage, I've made a career out of making people laugh. But you don't need to be an expert. Anyone has the power to make people smile, from your science teacher to your dog — and before we know it, we can find ourselves laughing at the most unexpected of moments.

> Making people laugh is one of the greatest feelings in the world.

Inel's Masterclass in Joke Writing

There are many techniques to help when writing a joke. Have fun with the process — and remember to laugh.

Telling a joke is like telling a story, and good jokes tend to have **FOUR NARRATIVE ELEMENTS**:

AN ARC: a beginning, middle and end

CHARACTERS: the subject of the joke

CONFLICT: a situation or problem faced by the characters

RESOLUTION: the punchline (top tip: the best jokes end on the point of highest tension!)

There are various **TYPES OF JOKES** built around this plan:

KNOCK-KNOCK
This type of joke imagines someone is knocking on the door of a house. When someone answers, they deliver the punchline, which is usually a **PUN**.

> Knock Knock!
> Who's there?
> Boo.
> Boo who?
> Don't cry, it's just a joke!

ANECDOTAL
These jokes are written based on someone's personal life. A good anecdotal joke uses a **METAPHOR**, which is when something is described that isn't literally true.

> Do you know the mushy, wet sludge you get underneath a car tyre when it's snowing? That's my dad's cooking!

ONE-LINERS
One-liners squeeze a setup and punchline into one thought. My favourite type of one-liners uses **MISDIRECTION**. This is when someone sets up a joke whose punchline seems predictable and obvious, and then deliver an entirely different punchline.

> School is so terrible. I hate spending my evenings doing homework... I knew I shouldn't have become a teacher!

JULY

WORLD YOUTH SKILLS DAY

THE JOY OF ENTREPRENURSHIP

Entrepreneur Andy Ayim

I'm an entrepreneur, which means I believe so much in my ideas that I've started businesses in order to bring them into the world.

I love having big ideas and even bigger goals. What a great imagination you need to have to think about using wooden propellers to transport people from one place to another. That is what the Wright brothers did when they built the first airplane. Or how about your favourite toys? From your bicycle to your board game, these things were created by entrepreneurs who started with an idea... and found a market for it!

Entrepreneurship can come from anywhere and anyone.

Being an entrepreneur means having a dream, inspiring people to believe your dream and then working together to make that dream a reality. What I love most about entrepreneurship is that it can come from anywhere and anyone. And being an entrepreneur means I have the privilege of inspiring others to chase their dreams one day, too.

Andy's Ideas Workshop

An ideas workshop is a dedicated time and place for coming up with new ideas. Do you have a great idea brewing? Don't worry if not — you will have one soon enough!

First, **MAKE A LIST**. In the first column, write down things you enjoy doing. In the second column, write down things you are good at. Is there any crossover?

Reflecting on your answers above, write down all the ideas that come to mind when you think about the things **YOU ENJOY DOING AND ARE GOOD AT.**

It's now time to get creative! **DRAW** what your idea could be. This is the fun part where, as entrepreneurs, we start to turn our thoughts into things.

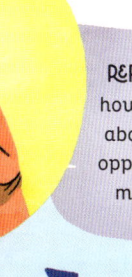

Finally, entrepreneurs are continuous learners, so it's important for us to be good at receiving **FEEDBACK**. You could ask your family or friends what they think about your idea, and whether they think there is a market for it.

REFLECT on the feedback and notice how it made you feel. The great thing about feedback is that it gives us an opportunity to improve our ideas and make them even better next time!

JULY

WORLD CHESS DAY

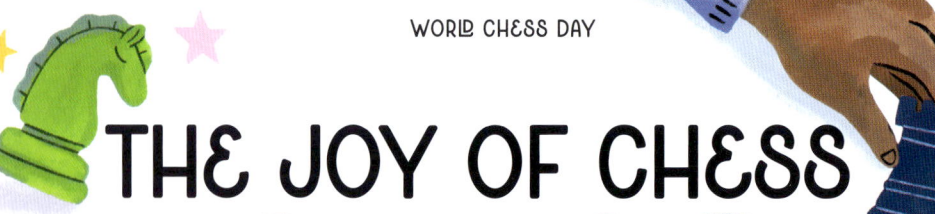

THE JOY OF CHESS

Grandmaster Maurice Ashley

Chess means everything to me. Many years ago, I played against a chess master from Hungary. We battled for hours, creating tricks and traps that we hoped the other person would fall for, until finally, the game ended in a tie.

Afterwards, we decided to compare notes, but I quickly realized that he did not speak any English and I even less Hungarian. No matter. We sat and started reviewing the game, and at certain points, we would stop to suggest other moves we thought might have been interesting to play.

Using only hand gestures, facial expressions, laughs and shakes of the head, we were able to easily communicate...

The language that we shared was the language of chess.

The language that we shared was the language of chess. That ability to share my passion with someone I cannot even speak to is one of the many reasons why I take joy from chess.

Maurice's Chess Moves

Chess has been spreading joy for over 1,500 years. It has lasted this long, I think, because of the simple yet enchanting shapes and movements of the various pieces.

The aim of the game is to defeat the enemy king, and to do that, one has to know how to properly use the rooks, knights, bishops, pawns and the mighty queen.

Each piece is special and moves in a magical way:

The **ROOK** moves in a straight line up, down or sideways.

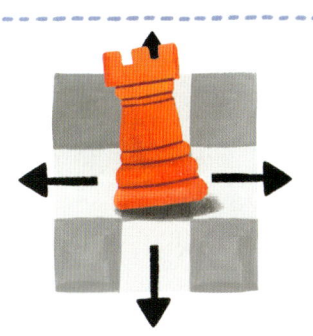

The **BISHOP** moves diagonally.

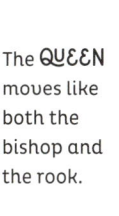

The **QUEEN** moves like both the bishop and the rook.

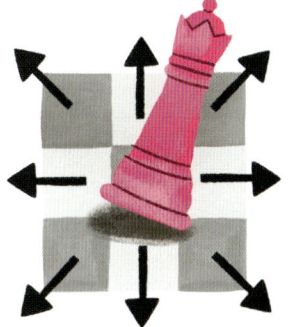

The **KNIGHT** moves in an 'L' shape.

The **PAWN** usually moves one square at a time, always forward like soldiers marching to war.

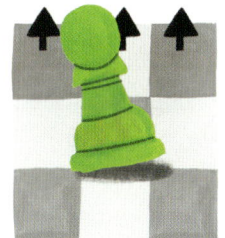

The **KING** moves only one step in any direction, and usually looks for safety in its castle unless needed in the end for battle.

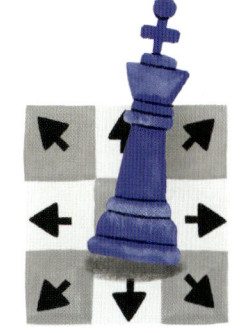

The word **CHECKMATE** signals a winner. It comes from an old Persian word meaning 'the king is helpless'.

JULY

INTERNATIONAL SELF-CARE DAY

THE JOY OF CREATIVE SELF-CARE

Artist Andrea Pippins

Taking the time to nurture my creativity not only brings me a lot of joy, but it's an important daily practice.

Self-care is an act of self-respect. It's about being mindful of what I need. For me, it's been the same since I was a child: being creative. I treasured growing a thought in my imagination and then bringing it to life. I remember feeling warm and at peace when I spent time drawing, and I still get that same fuzzy feeling today.

> Self-care is an act of self-respect.

The process of taking an idea out of my head and making it look exactly as I had imagined takes a bit of exploring and playing. Mixing colours with paint, trying new materials, listening to music while I draw or being inspired by something happening in the world are all ways I practise expressing my creativity — and by nurturing my creativity, I feed my soul.

Andrea's Guide to Creative Self-care

Making time each day to express our creativity brings us closer to our true selves and allows us to practise using our imaginations. Whether you like to build, garden, bake or paint, here are some ways you can nurture your creativity.

OPEN YOUR MIND
There is so much inspiration to be found at the LIBRARY. The next time you visit, explore a section you haven't considered before, or take out some new books on your favourite topic.

OPEN YOUR SOUL
Visiting GALLERIES gives me motivation to explore my own creativity — and studies have even shown that when you look at a beautiful piece of art, your brain releases a chemical that helps reduce stress.

TRY SOMETHING NEW
We are experimenting when we try something new. This is a form of play. I like COLLAGING a mix of papers and textiles to try something new in my work.

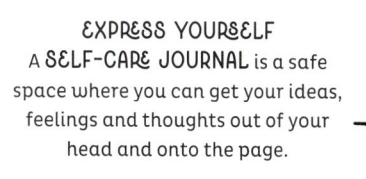

BE CURIOUS
Keep ASKING WHY and dig deep for answers. Consider getting multiple answers from different resources to unlock new ideas and ways of thinking about a subject.

EXPRESS YOURSELF
A SELF-CARE JOURNAL is a safe space where you can get your ideas, feelings and thoughts out of your head and onto the page.

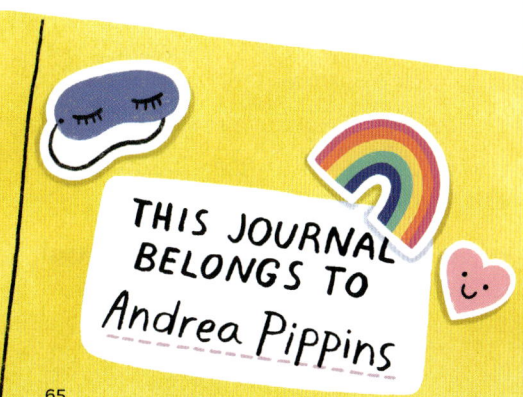

THIS JOURNAL BELONGS TO Andrea Pippins

JULY

SUMMER PARALYMPIC GAMES

THE JOY OF WHEELCHAIR RACING

My racing wheelchair provides me with an opportunity to be competitive. It has allowed me to move faster, to become stronger, to feel more empowered.

As I compete across the world, wheelchair racing has connected me to others. I have been fortunate enough to forge friendships with people from different nations, cultures and backgrounds. Some of the people I meet along the way live with different disabilities from mine, but we are one when we are lined up on the racing line: connected through our shared appreciation of the sport.

I love the speed my racing chair reaches. By using the strength of my upper body, wheelchair racing has given me some of the moments that make me feel most alive. I've come to realize that the word 'disabled' should not mean 'not able' because we are able. We are resilient. We can participate. What we need is an opportunity to shine... and wheelchair racing offers just that.

Wheelchair racing has given me some of the moments that make me feel most alive.

Anne's Anatomy of a Racing Wheelchair

Racing wheelchairs are not like everyday wheelchairs. Some people may be able to go fast in their everyday wheelchair, but they will never reach the same speeds as a sports wheelchair!

Athlete Anne Wafula Strike

SEAT
Racing wheelchairs are custom-built for each athlete's body measurements and abilities. Particular attention is paid to the seat to allow optimum body positioning: a 'sitting', 'tucked' or 'kneeling' position.

HANDLEBAR
The handlebar is used for steering and changes in direction. This is also where the brake lever sits, which activates the brake on the front wheel.

WHEELS
Racing chairs have two large wheels in the back and one smaller wheel in the front for balance. All three wheels are designed with either stainless steel spokes for rigidity or carbon fibre disks that can increase speed.

FRAME
The long, main tube that connects the front wheel to the back wheels is made of lightweight materials: aluminium or carbon fibre.

COMPENSATOR
The compensator acts like a rudder, holding the steering for the straight and bend so that my arms can focus on working the pushrim.

PUSHRIM
By rotating the pushrim, I can reach speeds of up to 30 kilometres an hour. This requires some serious upper body strength, as we aren't allowed any mechanical gears or levers to propel the chair.

AUGUST

WORLD PHOTOGRAPHY DAY

THE JOY OF PHOTOGRAPHY

Photographer and Filmmaker Nganji Mutiri

I've always loved capturing stories through a lens. All kinds of stories: the obvious ones and, more importantly, the unusual ones... The stories my eyes, mind and heart were missing in the mass media.

I thought, if nobody shows me different faces, emotions and places, I should document them myself — a mantra inspired by the novelist Toni Morrison.

Whether I'm in the Congo, where I grew up, or Belgium where I now live, my two favourite types of photographs happen when I either spontaneously pick up my camera and wander in the streets, resulting in always coming back home feeling more inspired than when I left; or when I call a person I've met before, we decide where we will meet, and then we create something magical together. If there is one thing that makes my heart sing, it's immortalising a moment in a photograph.

> If there is one thing that makes my heart sing, it's immortalising a moment in a photograph.

Moments by Nganji Mutiri

In this poem, I'm expressing the joy of photography, capturing moments in time from around the world.

Under a beauty-full black sky
Your eyes showed me where to go
How to talk
How to align the right energies

The slow gestures
On a fast lane

The collective decisions

The way inspirations
Stepped out of the car
Following us
For a little walk

The talk about
Whatever we felt
Comfortable with

The whisper asking to wait
For a crowd of fear to disappear

The silence before the first click

Trust appearing after the hundredth

Birds distracting some shots a bit

The renewed conversations
Deepening our thoughts

The tear
The contagious glimpses of vulnerability

The smile

The prodigious joy of our shared humanity

The laughter

The confidence to let a lens gently hold it

Like those precious seeds your elders
Told you to grow
Into empowering trees

Like those fruits
Feeding the knowing of having experienced
Similar emotions

Allowing even the most distant life-lover
To be reminded
That in each art-of-being-human
We singularly permit ourselves
To soul-fully inhabit
The same space
The same reflections

And

How that moment of short connection
Is the bright one
That nurtures
The roots of our wings.

AUGUST

WORLD FASHION DAY

THE JOY OF THREADS

Broadcaster Miquita Oliver

Clothes are full of stories. Stories of where they were found, where they've been worn before and where they'll be worn tomorrow.

That is why it's important for me to buy clothes that have lived. One of my most joyful memories is visiting charity shops with my grandmother (who I called Nanny), the ensuing hunt, and the fact that I had to trust what I was drawn to: shape, pattern, print, cut. What were my instincts telling me to listen to?

It's assumed that we just love a jacket or a pair of shoes because of the way they make us feel. I believe we're picking up on threads that run much deeper. I love kitten heels. They're smart, and they make me feel wonderful. But I also feel connected to something else, and it's my Nanny. It's my people putting on their Sunday best to leave their island and come to Britain. It's my mum and aunty Neneh wrapping their hair and dancing for their ancestors that came before us. Our clothes tell the world, "I know who I am, and I love myself." That's how important clothes are; how important our stories are.

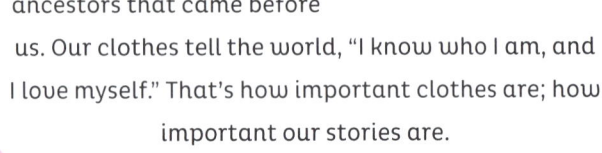

> *Our clothes tell the world, "I know who I am, and I love myself."*

Miquita's Story

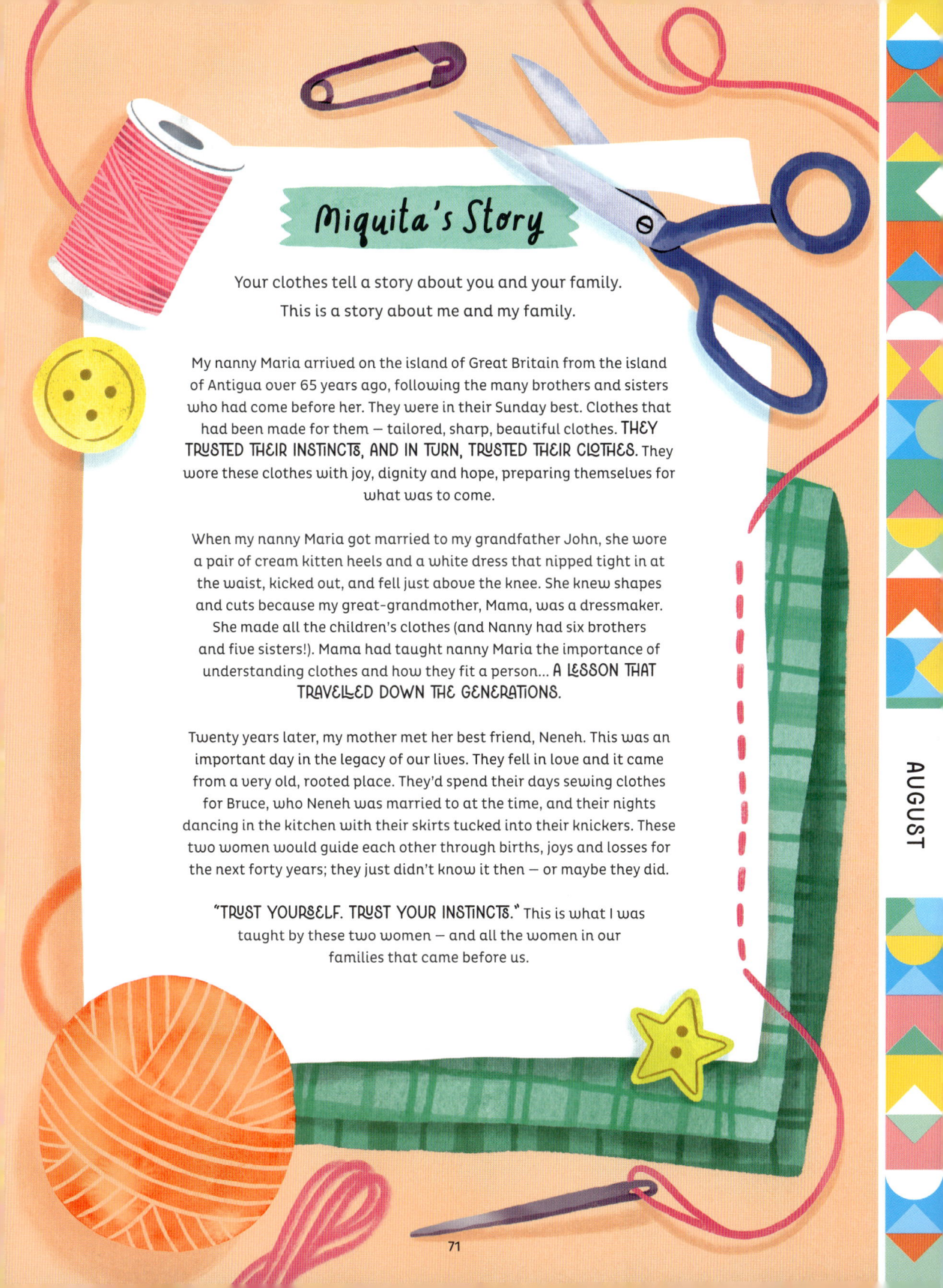

Your clothes tell a story about you and your family. This is a story about me and my family.

My nanny Maria arrived on the island of Great Britain from the island of Antigua over 65 years ago, following the many brothers and sisters who had come before her. They were in their Sunday best. Clothes that had been made for them — tailored, sharp, beautiful clothes. **THEY TRUSTED THEIR INSTINCTS, AND IN TURN, TRUSTED THEIR CLOTHES.** They wore these clothes with joy, dignity and hope, preparing themselves for what was to come.

When my nanny Maria got married to my grandfather John, she wore a pair of cream kitten heels and a white dress that nipped tight in at the waist, kicked out, and fell just above the knee. She knew shapes and cuts because my great-grandmother, Mama, was a dressmaker. She made all the children's clothes (and Nanny had six brothers and five sisters!). Mama had taught nanny Maria the importance of understanding clothes and how they fit a person... **A LESSON THAT TRAVELLED DOWN THE GENERATIONS.**

Twenty years later, my mother met her best friend, Neneh. This was an important day in the legacy of our lives. They fell in love and it came from a very old, rooted place. They'd spend their days sewing clothes for Bruce, who Neneh was married to at the time, and their nights dancing in the kitchen with their skirts tucked into their knickers. These two women would guide each other through births, joys and losses for the next forty years; they just didn't know it then — or maybe they did.

"TRUST YOURSELF. TRUST YOUR INSTINCTS." This is what I was taught by these two women — and all the women in our families that came before us.

AUGUST

INTERNATIONAL DOG DAY

THE JOY OF DOGS

House Dogge Founder Angela Medlin

When I was around eight years old, my dad brought home our first family dog in his jacket pocket. She was the tiniest puppy I had ever seen. We named her Penny, and she joined our adopted cat Smokey.

Penny bonded quickly with Smokey. There were no other dogs around, so she must have thought of herself as a cat. She even pooped in the cat's litter box and brushed up against our legs when she wanted attention. Eventually, she discovered her bark. I suspect it was a surprise to her that she was indeed a dog.

> Our dogs brought so much happiness to our family.

Penny became the matriarch to several other rescue dogs that joined our family over the next fifteen years. Our dogs brought so much happiness to our family, so much so that it eventually inspired me to create a pet brand, House Dogge, and today I love to research, design and develop products for the well-being of families, four legged and two-legged family members alike.

Angela's Reasons to Adopt a Dog

Finding yourself in the position to look after a furry friend is always an exciting time, but have you ever considered asking your caregivers to adopt a dog, instead of buying one new? There are so many advantages!

IT'S A GOOD DEED
Some dogs have had a sad start in life and are looking for a second chance. By adopting, you are giving a dog a safe and loving home.

YOU MIGHT FIND YOUR DREAM PET
By spending time with lots of different dogs, there's a good chance you'll find the one that fits into your family perfectly.

YOU'LL BE SUPPORTED
Rehoming centres carefully match dogs with the best new owners, offering advice, training and support throughout the adoption process.

YOU'LL ENCOURAGE OTHERS
When friends and family meet your adopted dog and hear about the dog of your dreams, they may think about adopting their next dog, too. Spread the doggy love!

AUGUST

CLASSICAL MUSIC MONTH

THE JOY OF CLASSICAL MUSIC

Cellist Sheku Kanneh-Mason

Classical music has played a significant role in my life. I grew up in a family where we'd listen to classical music at every opportunity... including the car!

I remember the journey to swimming practice because of Franz Schubert's piano quintet in A major. We'd pass by the same places at the same points in the music, and a hill had an immediate slope down from the top, which would line up with the recapitulation of the first movement. When I listen to this piece today, I am captivated by how it caught my imagination as a child.

Classical music has an incredible power over my mind and soul, and has given me many happy moments, like playing the cello at Prince Harry and Meghan Markle's wedding. I love being able to share the magical qualities of music with other musicians and an audience — it is a very special feeling that not many things can compare to.

> *Classical music has an incredible power over my mind and soul.*

Sheku's Anatomy of a Cello

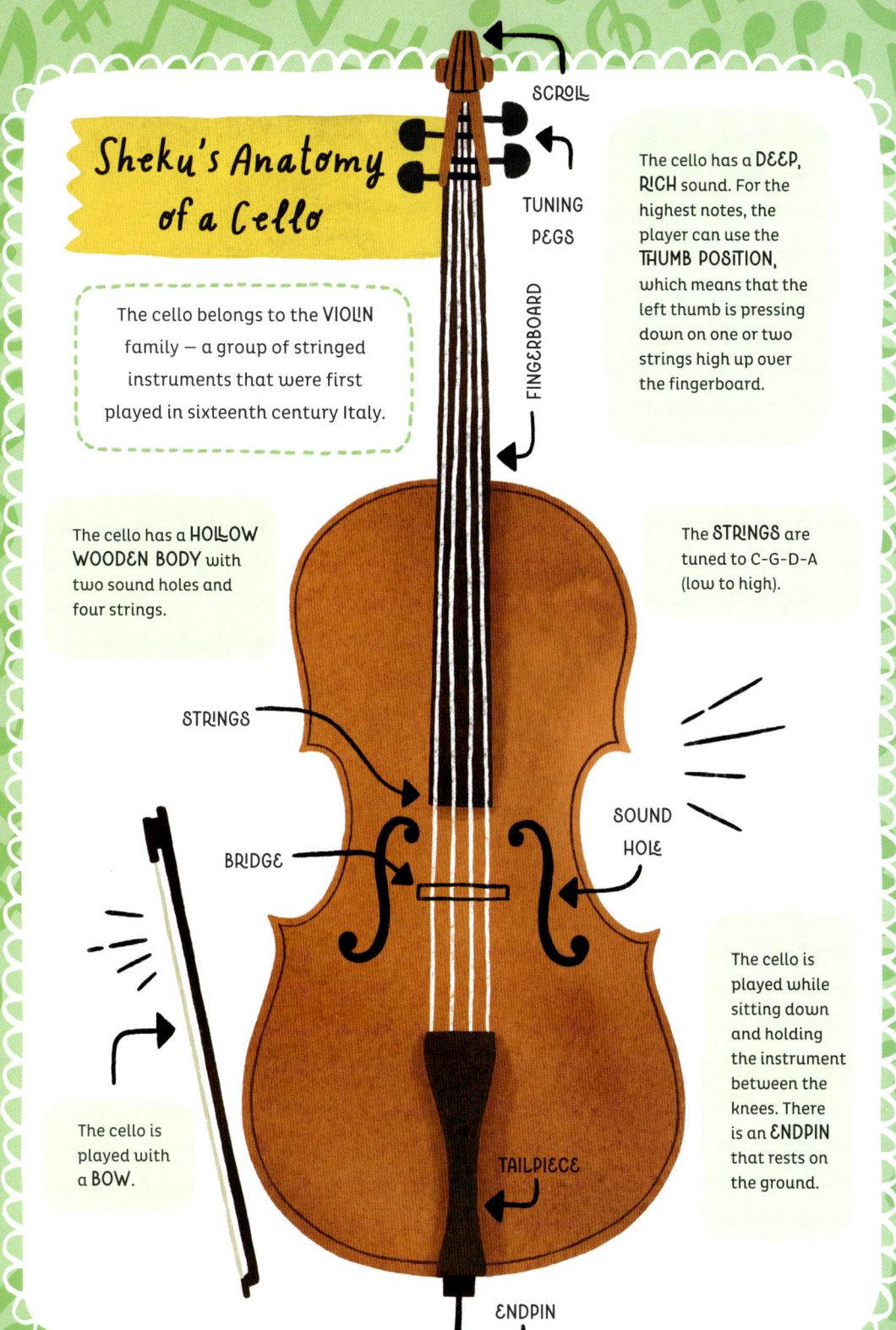

SCROLL

TUNING PEGS

FINGERBOARD

The cello has a DEEP, RICH sound. For the highest notes, the player can use the THUMB POSITION, which means that the left thumb is pressing down on one or two strings high up over the fingerboard.

The cello belongs to the VIOLIN family — a group of stringed instruments that were first played in sixteenth century Italy.

The cello has a HOLLOW WOODEN BODY with two sound holes and four strings.

The STRINGS are tuned to C-G-D-A (low to high).

STRINGS

BRIDGE

SOUND HOLE

The cello is played with a BOW.

The cello is played while sitting down and holding the instrument between the knees. There is an ENDPIN that rests on the ground.

TAILPIECE

ENDPIN

SEPTEMBER

75

MINDFULNESS DAY

THE JOY OF BREATHING

Breathwork Coach
Kathleen Booker

Oh, the JOY of breathing! I can hear you say, "But I breathe every day. What's the big deal?" Well, let me tell you of the wonders and power of your breath.

When I feel nervous, I take a breath and relax instantly. When I am studying a new subject, I take a breath and my mind opens for me to understand the topic. When I am taking an exam, I take a breath and find the relevant information from the depths of my brain. And if I find myself unable to, I take another breath.

Breathing is the greatest pleasure in life.

Breathing is the greatest pleasure in life. Reaching a state of calm can be as easy as taking a few deep breaths. This helps me when I am having a sad moment. When I feel sad thinking about my mum, who passed away, I take a deep breath in and remember the fun times we had together. A smile comes to my lips and makes the sad moment a little easier. I take a deep breath; I inhale peace and I exhale happiness.

Kathleen's Breathing Exercise

This calming breathing technique takes just a few minutes and can be done anywhere.

1. Make yourself as comfortable as you can. Whatever position you're in — sitting, standing or lying down — feel your body begin to relax, your shoulders and belly soften... feel more at ease in your body from head to toe.

2. Close your eyes, or look down at your nose.

3. Breathe in through your nose. Inhale gently, easily and deeply without moving your shoulders.

4. Breathe out through your mouth. Shall we do that again?

5. Breathe in through your nose. Slowly does it. Let your body enjoy taking a breath.

6. Breathe out through your mouth. Let it flow out gently. Notice how your body is beginning to relax.

7. Continue doing this for as long as you wish.

Can you feel the joy, the calm and relaxation in your body and mind? Breathwork is joy!

SEPTEMBER

INTERNATIONAL DAY OF DEMOCRACY

THE JOY OF DEMOCRACY

VOTE

Politician David Lammy

I grew up in London and things were hard for my family. We struggled to pay our bills, and when we wanted to be heard, we often felt like no one was listening.

That's why I got involved in politics. When I meet people around London today, I think of how I would like to have been listened to when I was young. When I stand up in the House of Commons, it brings me joy to know I am there on behalf of the people I speak to.

I believe every voice matters.

I believe every voice matters, and this is what fuels the passion in my politics. Politicians aren't supposed to come up with all the solutions — they're supposed to listen to people and help ensure the best ideas are used to change the world. If a young person watches me in parliament, in front of the prime minister, talking about issues that affect them, I know I have done my job well.

David's Democracy Lesson

A democracy is a country where the people choose their government. The world's largest democracy by population is India, followed by the United States and Indonesia.

The United Kingdom — where I am a member of Parliament — is also a democracy. Here's how my government is organized. A similar system is used in other countries, too, such as Australia, Canada and Japan.

MONARCH
The UK is officially ruled by a monarch (a king or queen) known as the executive, but real political power belongs to the legislative branch, known as Parliament.

HOUSES OF PARLIAMENT
Two groups of people meet to debate and vote on new laws. The groups are called houses.

The House of Commons: Members of Parliament (MPs) are elected by citizens every five years at a general election. MPs debate laws, and if more than half agree, they can make new laws or remove old laws.

The House of Lords: Lords can suggest amendments to laws and can vote against laws passed by the House of Commons.

GOVERNMENT
Most MPs belong to a political party, such as the Conservatives or the Green Party. If one party has more than half of the MPs, they form the government.

PRIME MINISTER
The leader of the political party with the most MPs becomes the prime minister. They are the most powerful politician in the country.

CABINET
The prime minister appoints some MPs, known as ministers, to be responsible for different policy areas, such as health.

AUTUMN EQUINOX

THE JOY OF AUTUMN FOOD

Chef Andi Oliver

There is a touch of magic about the autumnal larder. It's like nature has had its glad rags on for summer and has reached that point in the party where its head is thrown back in celebratory laughter!

Rich with the promise of comfort, autumn is a dreamy time in the kitchen: dark cobblers, bubbling pots of aromatic stews, bowls filled with tumbling black beans loaded with fried plantains, squashes rolled in spices and turned through oats and stock to make heartwarming skirlie, aromatic poached beetroots, fresh curds, zesty sorrel, roast garlic, gold rapeseed oil.

> Autumn is a dreamy time in the kitchen.

As the sunlight changes and the breeze starts to dance in the trees, I love to stand in my kitchen cooking from autumn's rich bounty — pickling cucumbers, making jams, caramelising onions. These are what my daydreams are made of!

Andi's Autumn Comfort: Spiced Squash and Caramelised Red Onion Skirlie

This is my favourite autumnal recipe. It was born from an old Scottish dish called skirlie, which is a savoury porridge. Think of it as oat risotto — both comforting and joyful!

INGREDIENTS

- 100g red onion, finely sliced
- 2 cloves garlic, grated
- 40ml olive oil
- 10g unsalted butter
- 2 tsp Caribbean curry powder
- 1/2 tsp chili flakes
- 200g butternut squash, peeled and diced
- 100g oats
- 350ml chicken stock
- Knob of butter
- Pinch salt, to season

METHOD

Preheat the oven to 190C/170C Fan/Gas 5.

Place a heavy-based frying pan over very low heat. Gently sauté the onions and garlic in butter and half of the oil for 20 minutes, until soft, sticky and golden.

Tip the remaining oil, curry powder and chili flakes into a bowl and mix to make a paste. Add in the diced butternut squash and stir well, ensuring it's thoroughly coated.

Slip the coated squash into an ovenproof dish and bake in the oven for 35 minutes, until the squash is tender but not mushy. Remove from the oven and add the squash to your frying pan, stirring it in with the onions and garlic.

Next stir in the oats, add the chicken stock, and cook it over medium heat for around 5 minutes. Throw in a knob of butter and a pinch of salt, and serve straight away to savour the joys of autumn!

SEPTEMBER

WORLD TOURISM DAY

THE JOY OF TRAVEL

Digital Creator Phil Calvert @philwaukee

At nine years old, I would spin a globe with my eyes closed and point to a random place. Once it landed, I would daydream for hours about what life was like there.

Now I'm a grown-up; I have been to 73 countries and 6 continents, and travelled by train, plane, car, boat, helicopter... and even camel! One of my favourite trips was to China, where I met my friend's grandmother. She was so excited because she had never met a Black person before. She made lots of different dishes for me to try — we ate bok choy (a type of Chinese cabbage) and chicken feet. In exchange, I traded her one of my favourite snacks: flamin' hot crisps. They were too spicy for her. (That's OK, more for me!)

For me, travelling is all about meeting new people, seeing new things and learning about new cultures. It truly is a beautiful way to learn about our world.

Travelling is a beautiful way to learn about our world.

Phil's Travel Tips

One of the most exciting aspects of travel is growing your understanding of other cultures. Here are a few tips for how you can be a respectful guest in a new country.

Learn about the different **CUSTOMS**. Some countries use different cutlery to eat, or use the bathroom differently, so do your homework to avoid sticking out like a sore thumb!

SEAT 2B

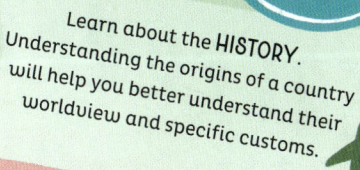

Learn about the **HISTORY**. Understanding the origins of a country will help you better understand their worldview and specific customs.

Learn a few phrases in the local **LANGUAGE**. It's nice to learn a handful of helpful words, even if just to show that you care enough to learn them.

HELLO!
Hola! Bonjour! Salve!

GOODBYE!
Adios! Au revoir! Arrivederci!

PLEASE
Por favor! S'il vous plaît! Bitte!

THANK YOU
Gracias! Merci! Danke!

CHEERS!
Salud! Santé! Prost!

welcome CHINA

ARRIVAL
WELCOME TO SCOTLAND

Ask **QUESTIONS**! If you're not sure, ask a local. People are often understanding and enjoy helping out travellers who care about their home and culture.

SEPTEMBER

83

NATIONAL HAIR DAY

THE JOY OF STYLING HAIR

Celebrity Hairstylist Yene Damtew

I've always been a hairstylist at heart. I grew up in a small city in California called La Palma, and from an early age you'd find me styling my doll's hair.

Hairstyling is like storytelling. We are storytellers; we're just telling someone else's story. There's nothing like listening to a client, bringing their vision to life and then watching them get up from my chair with a big smile on their face.

Hair is an expression of art and allows me to connect with many people to learn from and be inspired by. One of my greatest joys was styling Michelle Obama's hair for a magazine cover, where the world saw her wearing her natural curls for the first time. It was a defining moment not just for me or Ms Obama, but for the millions of women of colour who've been told their natural curls are not praiseworthy. I was so proud of that moment and all it stood for.

Hair is an expression of art.

Yene's Guide to Hair Care

All natural hair is beautiful, but no two people (or their hair!) are the same. We can all use a little guidance, and that's where a hairstylist comes in. Enter me!

It's best to figure out a hair regimen that works best for your hair and stick to it to see results. While everyone's regimen will be different, we can all follow similar steps to determine what works best for our hair.

TRIM THOSE ENDS
When you neglect the ends of your hair, they can split. It's ideal to get your ends trimmed by a professional every **6-8 WEEKS** to ensure that you continue on your healthy hair journey.

USE GOOD PRODUCTS
When choosing products, you'll want to find some that are both **HYDRATING AND NOURISHING** for the scalp and hair. I always recommend using conditioner every time you wash your hair. Be sure to coat the ends of the hair with conditioner, as the ends are the oldest and most fragile part of your hair.

REDUCE FRICTION DURING SLEEP
Movement during sleep can rub the hair and cause damage. Also, some fabrics can absorb moisture from the hair and scalp. To avoid these issues, it's a good idea to **REMOVE ANY TIGHT HAIRBANDS** before bed, and even use a smooth, silk or satin hair wrap or pillowcase.

WEAR PROTECTIVE STYLES
It's helpful to give your natural hair a break from time to time, and you can do that by wearing protective styles (styles that are easy to put in and take out). There are so many fun and beautiful protective styles to choose from, such as **KNOTLESS BRAIDS, TWO-STRAND TWISTS, FLAT TWISTS AND CROCHET BRAIDS.**

OCTOBER

85

WORLD ARCHITECTURE DAY

THE JOY OF BUILDINGS

Architect Sade Akinsanya

You'll often find me looking up, sketchbook in hand, taking inspiration from the incredible buildings in my home city of London.

Growing up, I spent my free time doodling away in a notepad. This creative streak led me to become an architect, using the skills I honed as a child, plus skills I've learned along the way, to design buildings. And the learning doesn't stop! I find my brain is constantly untangling puzzles in the form of constructions.

I'm forever in awe at the structures I pass by on my way to work in London, and I believe great buildings serve as the identity of a city. People in different parts of the world use different materials and styles based on what is available around them, what works in their climate and what their cultural identity is. Our connection to the environment around us is what brings us joy. Happiness is design that reflects our natural world, and therefore our place in it.

Our connection to the environment around us is what brings us joy.

London's Architecture Walk with Sade

When it comes to architectural excellence, London is bursting with innovative buildings and is blessed with a mixture of old and new.

ST PAUL'S CATHEDRAL is an oasis of calm within the bustling city. The architect behind its design, Sir Christopher Wren, created the famous hemispherical outer dome to dominate the skyline between 1675 and 1711, after the previous building was burned down in the Great Fire of London in 1666.

THE BRITISH LIBRARY was the largest public building constructed in twentieth century Britain. Architects Sir Colin St. John Wilson and MJ Long disguised the building's true size with a ceiling that gradually rises in increments to not overwhelm visitors.

Designed by Renzo Piano, **THE SHARD** was built as a place where people could live, work and relax. Today it stands as the tallest building in the United Kingdom, with a massive 11,000 glass panels — equivalent in area to eight football pitches!

Originally designed in the 1930s by the Sir Giles Gilbert Scott, **BATTERSEA POWER STATION** once provided one-fifth of London's electricity. Today it stands as the largest brick building in Europe and provides its community with homes, shops and restaurants.

OCTOBER

WORLD SPACE WEEK

THE JOY OF LOOKING UP

Space Scientist Dr. Maggie Aderin-Pocock

A clear night sky filled with stars is a wonderful sight. Looking up makes a difference to how I think about the world around me.

When I look up to the night sky, I remind myself that I'm following in the footsteps of our ancestors. Every culture has tried to understand what they are looking at. Some have written poems, others have built huge structures. (The world's first astronomical site, Nabta Playa, sits on African soil!) What they all had in common was that they were aware of the vastness of the universe.

Looking up makes a difference to how I think about the world around me.

It is remarkable to think about how small we truly are. After all, Earth only makes up about 0.0003 percent of the total mass of our solar system! We may be small, but we're part of something cosmic — and we get to see a part of the awe-inspiring spectacle just by looking up.

Dr. Maggie's Stargazing Tips

Take advantage of it getting darker earlier this month with some stargazing! Here are my five top stargazing tips:

CHECK THE DATE
The best time to go stargazing is the **DAYS AROUND THE NEW MOON**, when the sky is at its darkest. During these times, there is no bright moon to wash out the light from fainter stars, so you'll be able to see thousands more.

LOCATION, LOCATION, LOCATION
Find a spot where you can see as much of the night sky as possible. Make sure you're away from the streetlights, as their dazzle will stop you from seeing the stars. Your **BACK GARDEN** could work nicely, or perhaps walk with a trusted adult to your **LOCAL PARK**.

ADJUST YOUR EYES
To see the stars clearly, let your eyes get **'DARK ADAPTED'** by keeping them in the dark for around thirty minutes. You need to do this because the pupils of your eyes get bigger or smaller depending on the light levels.

LEARN AS YOU GO
There are many **STARGAZING APPS** that will help you instantly locate stars and planets. Just point your smartphone at the object you want to observe and the screen with tell you what you are looking at.

HAVE FUN!
I love to stargaze with my daughter, Lauren, who introduced me to a chocolate and marshmallow dessert called **S'MORES**. We eat those under the stars and have a relaxing evening with the cosmos together.

OCTOBER

WORLD MIGRATORY BIRD DAY

THE JOY OF BIRDS

Urban Birder David Lindo

Nothing fills my life with joy more than when I am watching birds. No matter where I am, whether it's in the middle of a city or on a remote island, the moment I see a bird, my spirit is lifted.

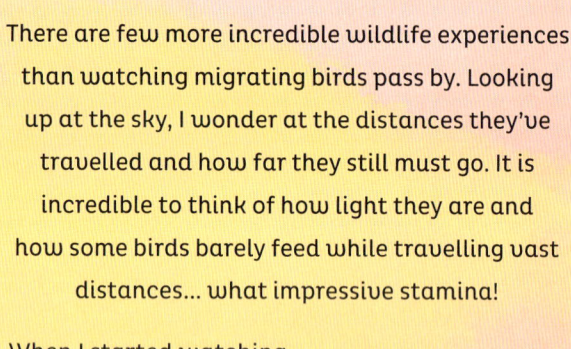

There are few more incredible wildlife experiences than watching migrating birds pass by. Looking up at the sky, I wonder at the distances they've travelled and how far they still must go. It is incredible to think of how light they are and how some birds barely feed while travelling vast distances... what impressive stamina!

When I started watching birds at the age of five, I made up my own names for the birds that I saw. Sparrows were baby birds; starlings were mummy birds; blackbirds were daddy birds. Today, I know the names for every bird I see, but one thing has never changed: the tingle in my toes when watching birds is the same as when I was five years old.

> The moment I see a bird, my spirit is lifted.

Bird Migration Q&A with David

Many birds make a long journey every year between their winter and summer homes. This journey is known as migration.

WHY DO BIRDS MIGRATE?
There is often more than one reason for birds to migrate, but it is usually for SURVIVAL. Birds want to avoid harsh weather and food shortages that winter brings to the regions where they breed, so they move to better areas to feed.

HOW LONG DOES MIGRATION TAKE?
A lot of it depends on how the bird gets their energy: small birds like WARBLERS use their fat reserves and can get from the UK to Africa in under three weeks. Larger birds like OSPREYS take over two months to make the same journey, as any extra fat would make them too heavy to fly!

WHICH BIRDS MIGRATE?
At least 4,000 species of birds migrate, which is about 40 percent of the world's total. Among the most well-known are the BAR-TAILED GODWITS. They have epic endurance — scientists recorded a godwit flying more than 7,500 miles for eleven days without stopping!

DO BIRDS MIGRATE ON THEIR OWN?
Many birds migrate in groups, known as flocks, to provide safety in numbers against predators. Some large birds, such as GEESE, fly in V formation. Each bird in the V gets some help from the one in front of it, due to the reduction of wind resistance... and this economical way of flying can help a bird fly 70 percent farther than one bird flying alone!

OCTOBER

NATIONAL FOSSIL DAY

THE JOY OF FOSSILS

Palaeontologist Dr. Lisa White

Anything can become a fossil, from the bones of a dinosaur to the feathers of a bird. Every fossil is unique, too — but what they all have in common is that they are all tangible connections to the past.

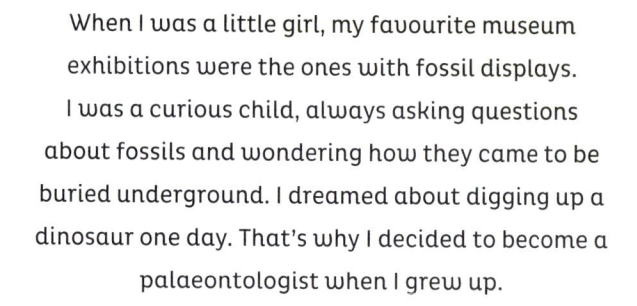

When I was a little girl, my favourite museum exhibitions were the ones with fossil displays. I was a curious child, always asking questions about fossils and wondering how they came to be buried underground. I dreamed about digging up a dinosaur one day. That's why I decided to become a palaeontologist when I grew up.

My work as a palaeontologist has taken me to many places around the world to collect and study fossils, including out to sea. Carrying my satchel of specialized tools, I have unearthed fossils that haven't been seen for millions of years... including parts from a dinosaur! I cannot express the thrill I feel when I am among the first to see and identify million-year-old fossils and offer the world an unparalleled insight into the history of the Earth.

> *I dreamed about one day digging up a dinosaur.*

Dr. Lisa's Dinosaur Fossil Dig

One of the questions I am often asked is how dinosaur fossils form. I'm here to tell you the answer...
Are you ready to join me on the dig?

Approximately 252 to 66 million years ago, **DINOSAURS** walked the Earth... until an **ASTEROID** struck!

The dinosaurs were buried quickly after their death in **SEDIMENTS** like sand or mud.

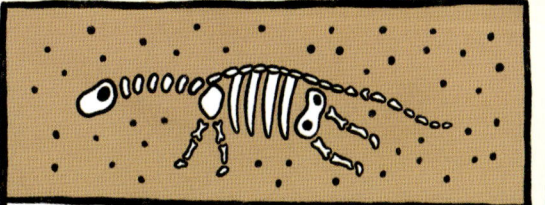

The soft part of the dinosaurs, like the muscles, rotted away — but the hard parts, like their **SKELETONS**, were left behind.

Over time, more and more layers of sediment covered the bones left behind. (That's why fossils are only found in **SEDIMENTARY ROCKS**.)

As more layers of sediment built up, the sediment around each bone compacted and became **ROCK**.

Water seeped into each bone and dissolved minerals carried by the water hardened in the spaces of the bone. The bone was then preserved in the surrounding rock. This is a **FOSSIL**.

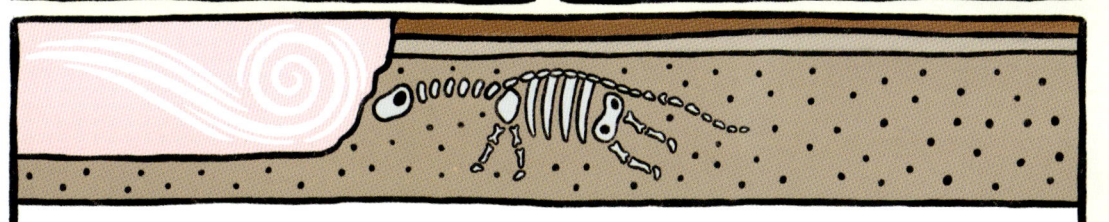

Then, over millions of years, the fossil rose to the surface as earth and sediment were worn away by **EROSION**... and now waits to be discovered by **PALAEONTOLOGISTS** like me!

OCTOBER

INTERNATIONAL ARCHAEOLOGY DAY

THE JOY OF ARCHAEOLOGY

Archaeologist Dr. Ayana Flewellen

History is all around us, and searching for the history buried beneath us is my favourite pastime.

Growing up, my mother would often take me to the American History Museum in Washington, D.C. I spent hours reading every display board, taking in the wonders of every artifact. As I grew older, I learnt that I could become one of the people discovering the objects that I viewed in museums with such amazement.

One of my most memorable archaeological experiences was excavating the Estate Little Princess, a nineteenth-century plantation where enslaved people lived and laboured. I unearthed the fragments of a ceramic doll, and as I rubbed my fingers against the smooth porcelain I, for the first time, imagined the possibility of play even under the direst circumstances. While my work is clouded in some of the most challenging aspects of human history, there's great pride and joy in finding a new piece of history.

There's great pride and joy in finding a new piece of history.

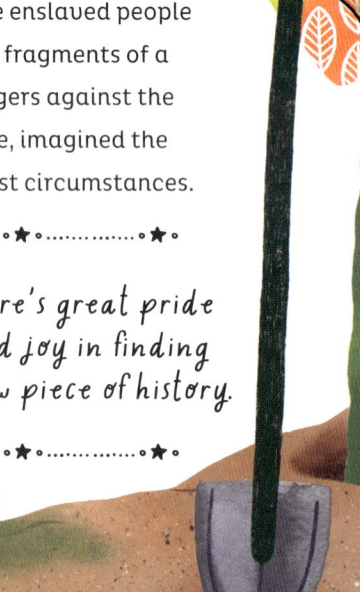

Dr. Ayana's Remarkable Finds

My most important dig to date was at the Estate Little Princess, a Danish plantation site on the island of St Croix, a US Virgin Island in the Caribbean, where the team and I found objects from enslaved peoples who once lived on the island.

My work begins once a site is located. I dig slowly and carefully, using tools like trowels and brushes to uncover artifacts. It's then time to ask questions such as, "WHAT WAS IT MADE FROM?" and "WHAT WAS IT USED FOR?" to help us to understand the past.

PEWTER SPOON
The tip of a pewter spoon was found and it didn't look like it came from the Caribbean. A trip to the library revealed that enslaved Africans often BROUGHT THEIR POSSESSIONS WITH THEM to a plantation, offering clues to how people kept their individuality within a system designed to strip them of it.

GLASS BOTTLE STOPPER
This glass bottle stopper had a closing design based on a glass marble. Elders shared stories about CHILDHOOD GAMES and how they got into trouble with their parents, because they would break the bottles open to use the stopper as a marble. This type of archaeological research is known as 'oral history'.

PORCELAIN DOLLS
Coming across FRAGMENTS OF DOLLS while digging can be a bit scary: an arm here, a leg there. Dolls from this time often had bodies made from stuffed canvas sacks, which don't preserve well. However, porcelain parts preserve very well, and offer us an insight into what children played with at the time.

BONE BUTTONS
We found many finished bone buttons, but no larger, flat pieces of bone from which the buttons would have been carved. This told us that enslaved people on the island were likely BUYING OR TRADING BUTTONS, not making them.

OCTOBER

NATIONAL STEM DAY

THE JOY OF STEM

Cofounder of Stemettes
Dr. Anne-Marie Imafidon

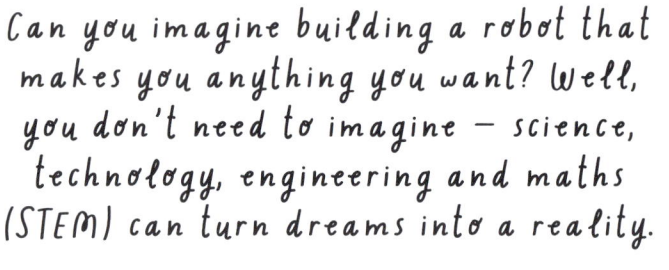

Can you imagine building a robot that makes you anything you want? Well, you don't need to imagine — science, technology, engineering and maths (STEM) can turn dreams into a reality.

We all have the tools to create solutions to big and small problems. Applying our knowledge of STEM allows us to imagine anything, and then make it! STEM encourages us to explore our imaginations, ask questions, solve problems and get creative.

And I love getting creative to not only solve my problems, but the problems of people I don't know. I love that whatever I create it to do, it's able to do that again, and again and again in the same way, so each person gets use of it, too, without me having to be there. Once you are done imagining, you can get on and create.

> *I love getting creative to solve problems.*

Dr. Anne-Marie's STEM Challenge

It's time to learn through exploration! Turn the materials you would normally send out in your recycling into something that you can design, build and test… like a boat!

MATERIALS
- a large piece of cardboard
- duct tape
- two plastic bottles with caps

METHOD

1. Cut out a small cardboard rectangle and cover it in duct tape.

2. Tape two plastic water bottles side by side to the bottom of the cardboard.

3. Cut out a small cardboard triangle and cover it with duct tape.

4. Tape the triangle to the boat to make a sail.

TEST
Fill a container, or your sink, with water. Does your boat float? Do you think the boat will still float with your toy on top? Test it out! Experiment with the number of toys the boat will hold before it starts to sink under the water.

NOVEMBER

WORLD ADOPTION DAY

THE JOY OF OWNING YOUR VOICE

Podcasters Sandria Washington and Dr. Samantha Coleman

After years of friendship, we never imagined having a podcast together — especially one that provided a safe space to discuss Black adoption stories.

Adoption wasn't talked about in our families when we were growing up. It was a secret. We learned as adults that we were adopted and wondered, "Are there more Black adoptees like us?" So we created a podcast and used the power of telling our stories to find out! After all, the human voice is a powerful instrument.

What did we discover? The joy of connecting with people and creating community. The joy of supporting others in telling their stories and helping them feel heard. The joy of owning our voices and thereby giving others permission to do the same.

The human voice is a powerful instrument.

Sandria's and Dr. Samantha's Guide to Owning Your Voice

The world needs your voice, too. If there are things in your neighbourhood or school that you want to change, speak up! One voice makes a difference. You could always do what we did and grab a friend to tackle the scary stuff together.

RECOGNIZE YOUR VOICE IS VALUABLE
It can be easy to tell ourselves that our thoughts and opinions are not as important as others. When we do this, we minimize what we bring to a conversation. Instead of measuring your worth against others, **BELIEVE IN WHAT YOU HAVE TO SAY.** You matter. Your words matter.

BE COMFORTABLE BEING UNCOMFORTABLE
Being uncomfortable is how we grow and learn. When we push ourselves to do things we thought we were incapable of, our self-confidence skyrockets! The only person holding you back is you. **STRETCH YOURSELF TO SPEAK UP AND SPEAK OUT.**

FIND YOUR COMMUNITY
Nothing brings people together like a common cause. Think about who would benefit the most from the cause you care about. Once you identify those people, **ASK QUESTIONS AND LISTEN TO THEIR PERSPECTIVES.**

STICK TO YOUR VALUES
Others may attempt to sway your ideas and decisions in a way that's not in your best interest. In these moments, try to do what is best and right for you. **REMEMBER WHO YOU ARE, WHERE YOU CAME FROM AND WHAT YOU STAND FOR.**

MAKE IT COUNT
It's a privilege for people to connect with you and listen to what you have to say. Your voice is your power, so recognize your influence and **CHOOSE TO MAKE AN IMPACT IN POSITIVE WAYS.**

NOVEMBER

GLOBAL DAY OF ACTION FOR CLIMATE JUSTICE

THE JOY OF ACTIVISM

Climate Justice Activist Vanessa Nakate

Pushing for change is hard, but activism is about imagining and aspiring towards a better future. For me, it's about envisioning a society in which everyone has access to food, education, clean air and a stable climate.

I grew up in Uganda and saw the impacts of the climate crisis firsthand. People have lost their lives and livelihoods because of flooding and landslides. I have learned that the people can build a fairer and more just world that works for all of us.

I find joy with my fellow activists. We have times when we find the lack of change demoralising, but there is no work more inspiring than fighting to save our collective future. I also find joy in my faith. It has taught me not to throw away my fearless confidence, for it carries a great and glorious reward. It has given me hope — now I believe that another world with a steady climate is not only necessary, but also possible.

> There is no work more inspiring than fighting to save our collective future.

Vanessa's Climate Justice Trailblazers

Climate change is the biggest challenge facing our global society, which means there are lots of opportunities to make a difference — and I'm not making a difference on my own!

ELIZABETH WANJIRU WATHUTI founded the GREEN GENERATION INITIATIVE, an organization that nurtures children to love nature from a young age. She has planted over 30,000 TREE SEEDLINGS in Kenya so far!

ERIC NJUGUNA started his climate activism in 2017 after extreme droughts impacted his school's water supply. He is a youth climate justice organizer with environmental groups such as ZERO HOUR and FRIDAYS FOR FUTURE KENYA and speaks out on the consequences of climate change.

Hailing from the Democratic Republic of the Congo, GUILLAUME KALONJI founded the DRC arm of the RISE UP MOVEMENT, an organization that gives African climate activists a platform for their voices to be heard by the world.

LEAH NAMUGERWA uses SOCIAL MEDIA to spread her activism. Her incredible work spans from leading tree planting campaigns to starting a petition to enforce a PLASTIC BAG BAN in her home country of Uganda.

NOVEMBER

NATIONAL RUGBY DAY

THE JOY OF RUGBY

Rugby Football Union Chairman Tom Ilube

I started playing rugby when I was ten years old, and I loved the game right from the start. Not just because I was good at it (my coach said I was a talented winger!), but because it allowed me to become part of a team.

As I grew up, it became clear that I wasn't quite good enough to play rugby for my country, England. But the brilliant thing about rugby, I realized, is that there are lots of ways to be part of the team — whether that's as a referee, a coach, or even help run the whole game like I do today.

Since the age of ten, I've believed rugby is the best sport in the world, and I felt so proud when I was appointed the first Black chairman of the Rugby Football Union. I'd love to go back to my ten-year-old self and tell that little boy that one day, he'd be responsible for the sport he held so dear. Life doesn't get much more joyful than that!

> Rugby is the best sport in the world.

Tom's Guide to Rugby Union

Rugby union, commonly known as rugby, originated in Warwickshire, England, in 1823. Today, rugby is played in more than 120 countries around the world.

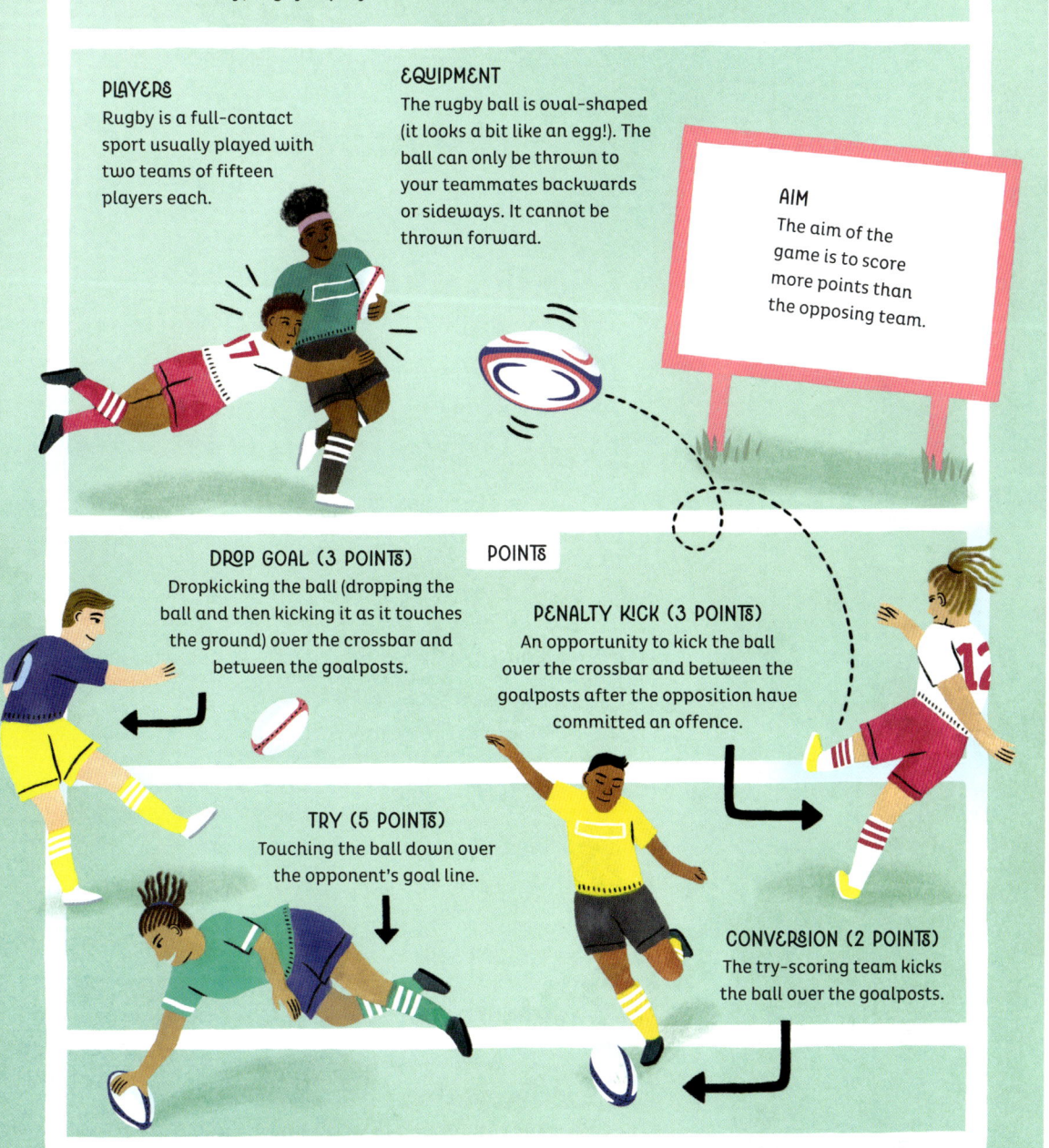

PLAYERS
Rugby is a full-contact sport usually played with two teams of fifteen players each.

EQUIPMENT
The rugby ball is oval-shaped (it looks a bit like an egg!). The ball can only be thrown to your teammates backwards or sideways. It cannot be thrown forward.

AIM
The aim of the game is to score more points than the opposing team.

POINTS

DROP GOAL (3 POINTS)
Dropkicking the ball (dropping the ball and then kicking it as it touches the ground) over the crossbar and between the goalposts.

PENALTY KICK (3 POINTS)
An opportunity to kick the ball over the crossbar and between the goalposts after the opposition have committed an offence.

TRY (5 POINTS)
Touching the ball down over the opponent's goal line.

CONVERSION (2 POINTS)
The try-scoring team kicks the ball over the goalposts.

NOVEMBER

WORLD WILDLIFE CONSERVATION DAY

THE JOY OF ANIMALS

Zookeeper and Wildlife Educator
Jungle Jordan

The human-animal bond is unlike any other. Animals bring unconditional love and happiness into our lives, and caring for my zoo's animals is the greatest joy in the world.

I was diagnosed with attention deficit hyperactivity disorder (ADHD) as a child. I felt different from my friends, but I soon learned ADHD was my superpower. It made me curious, and it means I can stay focused on a task for hours. At five years old, you'd find me walking around my local zoo sharing animal facts with anyone who would listen. I found a second home at the zoo, and at eleven years old, I became the youngest volunteer in the zoo's history.

Caring for my zoo's animals is the greatest joy in the world.

From providing care to protecting endangered species, zoos are so much more than a collection of animals. They are places for education. They are places for research. They are places for conservation. Without them, the world would be, and would increasingly become, a much poorer place.

Jordan's Top Conservation Stories

Good zoos are powerful forces for conservation, and some of the world's most extraordinary species would not be surviving without them.

The **AMUR LEOPARD** is the most critically endangered leopard. There are only around 100 in the wild, but zoos are changing that with **CONSERVATION BREEDING PROGRAMS**. 200 Amur leopards exist in zoos worldwide and are being encouraged to reproduce, with the aim of one day releasing the offspring in the wild.

Cutting down of forests, also known as deforestation, reduced the **GOLDEN LION TAMARIN'S** population to just a few hundred in its native home of Brazil. That was until nearly 150 **ZOOS JOINED FORCES** to save the species. Today, about a third of these wild monkeys are descendants of tamarins raised in human care.

In the 1980s, there were fewer than 30 **CALIFORNIA CONDORS** left in the wild. They were taken to zoo breeding centres and in 1988, the first zoo-bred condor chick hatched. Four years later, the first condors were released, and there are now thought to be around 330 **WILD BIRDS FLYING** across the United States.

In the 1960s, the **GIANT TORTOISE** population on the Galápagos Islands was reduced to just 15 individuals. The San Diego zoo sent their tortoise Diego to be part of a Galápagos breeding programme. Diego is believed to have fathered around 800 tortoises. That's 40 percent of today's wild population!

INTERNATIONAL MOUNTAIN DAY

THE JOY OF MOUNTAINS

Adventurer Sibusiso Vilane

Growing up in rural South Africa, I knew little of the world outside my village. But I had a thirst for the outdoors and, at the age of twenty-six, I climbed my first mountain: the Drakensberg range. Standing at the summit, I looked down and felt a massive sense of achievement.

Fast forward seven years, and I had made it to the top of the world: Mount Everest. Reaching the top of a mountain is an incredible experience. The joy of being up on a mountain can never be duplicated.

I climb because of the way it makes me feel. I feel free and liberated when climbing up, and I feel a sense of clarity when walking down. And each climb takes me to the next step. The next mountain. The next source of joy.

> Reaching the top of a mountain is an incredible experience.

WAY TO EVEREST

Sibusiso's Journey to the Top of the World

I have climbed the highest peak on each of the seven continents, known as the 'Seven Summits', which is no mean feat! It took training, proper equipment and careful planning.

MOUNT KILIMANJARO
Continent: Africa

Elevation: 5,895 metres

The climb up Mount Kilimanjaro in Tanzania ventures through several habitats — one moment I was in a rainforest with a colobus monkey, the next, I was alone on a snowy mountain!

ACONCAGUA
Continent: South America

Elevation: 6,961 metres

Aconcagua is in the Andes Mountains and has unpredictable weather due to its distance from the equator — it can change from bright sunshine to freezing gales in a split second!

PUNCAK JAYA
Continent: Oceania

Elevation: 4,884 metres

Despite having the lowest elevation out of the seven summits, Puncak Jaya on the island of New Guinea was the most technically difficult and involved a lot of rock climbing.

MOUNT EVEREST
Continent: Asia

Elevation: 8,849 metres

Located in the Himalayas, Mount Everest's summit had one-third of the air pressure at sea level, significantly reducing my ability to breathe in enough oxygen.

MOUNT ELBRUS
Continent: Europe

Elevation: 5,642 metres

Standing in the Caucasus Mountain range, Mount Elbrus is the tallest mountain in Europe, and is covered in snow all year round (so I needed to pack my thermals!).

MOUNT VINSON
Continent: Antarctica

Elevation: 4,892 metres

Mount Vinson was more of a snow trudge than a technical climb, but the Ellsworth Mountain region's remoteness and low temperatures meant it was still very tough.

DENALI
Continent: North America

Elevation: 6,190 metres

Located near the Alaska Range, Denali has five massive glaciers on its slopes, and some of the glaciers are more than 30 miles long. The crampons and ice axe were out in full force!

DECEMBER

WINTER EQUINOX

THE JOY OF PLANT HISTORY

Plant Historian Advolly Richmond

Have you ever looked at a plant and wondered about where it came from? Did it arrive in the country as a seed, a bulb or even a live plant? Who introduced it and from where?

As a plant historian, it's my job to ask these questions — and find out the answers if I can! Every plant has a story to tell, and my favourite time to discover these stories is in winter. It's a season where there's not much use being outside in the garden, so I hunker down with my research.

> Every plant has a story to tell.

My home is filled with precious books that help me tell a plant's story. For example, did you know that the flower emblem of Los Angeles is *Strelitzia reginae*, also known as the bird of paradise, but it actually came from South Africa over a hundred years ago? When I discover these gems, I feel a bit like a detective — I've found the missing clue or piece of the puzzle!

Advolly's History of Vanilla

Vanilla comes from the fruit or long beans of the climbing orchid *Vanilla planifolia*. It's my favourite plant, and one that has a very long and fascinating history.

Modern-day Mexico is the birthplace of vanilla. Over 800 years ago, the AZTECS used it to flavour their chocolate. They called it TLILXOCHITL (pronounced tea-so-shill), which means 'black flower'.

In the eighteenth century, the orchid was transported to other countries in attempts to cultivate vanilla. It proved unsuccessful, though, because the plant's natural pollinator, the tiny Mexican MELIPONA BEE, had been left behind.

Two centuries later in 1841, on the tiny island of Réunion in the Indian Ocean, a twelve-year-old enslaved boy called EDMOND ALBIUS discovered how to hand-pollinate the flower using small, sharp bamboo sticks and the flip of the thumb.

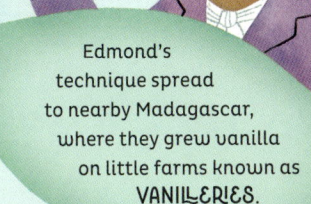

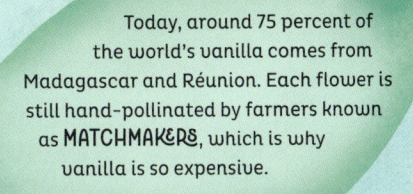

Edmond's technique spread to nearby Madagascar, where they grew vanilla on little farms known as VANILLERIES.

Today, around 75 percent of the world's vanilla comes from Madagascar and Réunion. Each flower is still hand-pollinated by farmers known as MATCHMAKERS, which is why vanilla is so expensive.

DECEMBER

CHRISTMAS

THE JOY OF MAKING

Crafter Nerrisa Pratt

Growing up, my parents encouraged my creativity, and I have fond memories of decorating cakes and cards for our loved ones, especially at Christmastime.

As I got older, I embraced my creativity, and by working hard at my hobbies, I managed to turn 'making things' into a career — something I never thought would be possible. From designing cushions and lampshades to sewing plant pot covers and bags, I feel so lucky that 'work' for me is crafting the day away with my cat, Milo, by my side.

Being able to make things with my hands is my superpower, and it's an ode to little Nerrisa every time I make something. Making is a calming and relaxing experience that sparks real joy, and there's truly no better feeling than when someone tells me they like one of my craft items and I can proudly say, "Thanks, I made it myself!"

> It's an ode to little Nerrisa every time I make something.

Christmas Crafting with Nerrisa

Making a Christmas card for your best friend is a great way to show them how much they mean to you - and this 'pop up' cracker is one of my favourite cards to make.

MATERIALS
- One sheet of festive wrapping paper
- A pencil
- A pair of scissors
- One A4 piece of coloured card
- A glue stick
- Any decorative items

TO MAKE THE CRACKER

1. Take the Christmas wrapping paper and turn it over. On the plain side, draw a Christmas cracker no bigger than the A4 piece of coloured card.

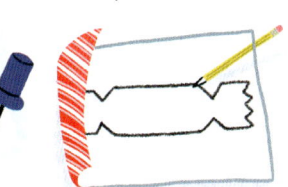

2. Carefully cut around the drawing, then place the cracker to the side.

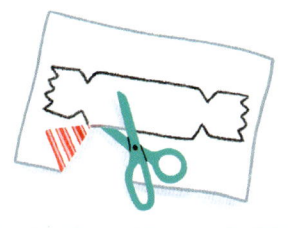

TO MAKE THE CARD

1. Take the A4 piece of coloured card and fold it in half.

2. Open the card, place your cracker in the centre, then fold the card closed with the cracker inside.

3. Open the card again, run a line of glue along the left-hand side of the cracker, and stick it in place. Repeat on the right-hand side.

4. Write your message on the cracker, then close the card. Now it's time to decorate! You could use anything from coloured crayons to glitter.

5. As Christmas approaches, hand the card to your best friend. When they open it, the cracker will 'pop up'. Merry Christmas!

DECEMBER

In memory of WFW, aka Dr. Mom and Jason Tyler. You embodied joy in this realm, and your energy dances infinitely in our hearts and into the divine. Thank you for your everlasting love. — J.W.

For my family, my biggest joy in the world. — J.O.

MAGIC CAT PUBLISHING

A Year of Black Joy © 2023 Lucky Cat Publishing Ltd
Compilation and text excluding individual contributions © 2023 Jamia Wilson
Illustrations © 2023 Jade Orlando
First Published in 2023 by Magic Cat Publishing, an imprint of Lucky Cat Publishing Ltd, Unit 2 Empress Works, 24 Grove Passage, London E2 9FQ, UK
EU Authorised Representative Magic Cat Publishing, an imprint of Lucky Cat Publishing Ltd, PAKTA svetovanje d.o.o., Stegne 33, Ljubljana, Slovenia
This paperback edition first published in 2025

Individual contributions: Davalois Fearon's text for 'Choreographers Day' © 2023 Davalois Fearon; Hazel Gardiner's text for 'International Flower Day' © 2023 Hazel Gardiner; David Hale Sylvester's text for 'National Hugging Day' © 2023 David Hale Sylvester; Nathan Holder's text for 'International Day of Education' © 2023 Nathan Holder; Lady Phyll's text for 'LGBT+ History Month' © 2023 Lady Phyll; Tolga Aktas's text for 'World Wetlands Day' © 2023 Tolga Aktas; Dr. Raven Baxter's text for 'International Day of Women and Girls in Science' © 2023 Dr. Raven Baxter; Dr. John McWhorter's text for 'International Mother Language Day' © 2023 Dr. John McWhorter; Patrice Lawrence's text for 'World Book Day' © 2023 Patrice Lawrence; Tabitha St.Bernard-Jacobs's text for 'International Women's Day' © 2023 Tabitha St.Bernard-Jacobs; Amanda Yee's text for 'Spring Equinox' © 2023 Amanda Yee; Lemn Sissay's text for 'World Poetry Day' © 2023 Lemn Sissay; Alex Wallace's text for 'World Meteorological Day' © 2023 Alex Wallace; Laura Henry-Allain's text for 'Diversity Month' © 2023 Laura Henry-Allain; Michelle Ogundehin's text for 'National Decorating Month' © 2023 Michelle Ogundehin; Tatyana Fazlalizadeh's text for 'World Art Day' © 2023 Tatyana Fazlalizadeh; Dr. Ronx Ikharia's text for 'World Immunisation Week' © 2023 Dr. Ronx Ikharia; Tayshan Hayden-Smith's text for 'National Gardening Week' © 2023 Tayshan Hayden-Smith; Jade Orlando's text for 'National Drawing Day' © 2023 Jade Orlando; Gillian Burke's text for 'International Day for Biological Diversity' © 2023 Gillian Burke; Chantale Zuzi's text for 'World Day for Cultural Diversity for Dialogue and Development' © 2023 Chantale Zuzi; Dr. Bethanie Edwards's text for 'World Ocean Day' © 2023 Dr. Bethanie Edwards; Samantha Foxx's text for 'Summer Equinox' © 2023 Samantha Foxx; Dr. Birgitta Johnson's text for 'World Music Day' © 2023 Dr. Birgitta Johnson; Dr. Marie Lahai's text for 'World Social Media Day' © 2023 Dr. Marie Lahai; Inel Tomlinson's text for 'International Joke Day' © 2023 Inel Tomlinson; Andy Ayim's text for 'World Youth Skills Day' © 2023 Andy Ayim; Maurice Ashley's text for 'World Chess Day' © 2023 Maurice Ashley; Andrea Pippins's text for 'International Self-Care Day' © 2023 Andrea Pippins; Anne Wafula Strike's text for 'Summer Paralympic Games' © 2023 Anne Wafula Strike; Nganji Mutiri's text for 'World Photography Day' © 2023 Nganji Mutiri; Miquita Oliver's text for 'World Fashion Day' © 2023 Miquita Oliver; Angela Medlin's text for 'International Dog Day' © 2023 Angela Medlin; Sheku Kanneh-Mason's text for 'Classical Music Month' © 2023 Sheku Kanneh-Mason; Kathleen Booker's text for 'Mindfulness Day' © 2023 Kathleen Booker; David Lammy's text for 'International Day of Democracy' © 2023 David Lammy; Andi Oliver's text for 'Autumn Equinox' © 2023 Andi Oliver; Phil Calvert's text for 'World Tourism Day' © 2023 Phil Calvert; Yene Damtew's text for 'National Hair Day' © 2023 Yene Damtew; Sade Akinsanya's text for 'World Architecture Day' © 2023 Sade Akinsanya; Maggie Aderin-Pocock's text for 'World Space Week' © 2023 Maggie Aderin-Pocock; David Lindo's text for 'World Migratory Bird Day' © 2023 David Lindo; Dr. Lisa White's text for 'National Fossil Day' © 2023 Dr. Lisa White; Dr. Ayana Flewellen's text for 'International Archaeology Day' © 2023 Dr. Ayana Flewellen; Anne-Marie Imafidon's text for 'National STEM Day' © 2023 Anne-Marie Imafidon; Sandria Washington's and Dr. Samantha Coleman's text for 'World Adoption Day' © 2023 Sandria Washington and Dr. Samantha Coleman; Vanessa Nakate's text for 'Global Day of Action for Climate Justice' © 2023 Vanessa Nakate; Tom Ilube's text for 'National Rugby Day' © 2023 Tom Ilube; Jordan Veasley's text for 'World Wildlife Conservation Day' © 2023 Jordan Veasley; Sibusiso Vilane's text for 'International Mountain Day' © 2023 Sibusiso Vilane; Advolly Richmond's text for 'Winter Equinox' © 2023 Advolly Richmond; Nerrisa Pratt's text for 'Christmas' © 2023 Nerrisa Pratt

The right of Jamia Wilson to be identified as the author of this work and Jade Orlando to be identified as the illustrator of this work and the right of the individual contributors to be identified as the authors of their respective contributions have been asserted in accordance with the Copyright, Designs and Patents Act, 1988.

No part of this publication may be reproduced, stored in a retrieval system, or transmitted, in any form or by any means, electrical, mechanical, photocopying, recording or otherwise without the prior written permission of the publisher or a licence permitting restricted copying.

A catalogue record for this book is available from the British Library.

ISBN 978-1-917366-00-7

The illustrations in this book were created using gouache, ink and digital media
Set in Pluto, Rocking Horse and Kindred

Published by Rachel Williams and Jenny Broom
Designed by Nicola Price and Sophie Gordon
Edited by Helen Brown

Manufactured in China

9 8 7 6 5 4 3 2 1

MIX
Paper | Supporting responsible forestry
FSC® C104723

The publisher would like to thank every person who shared their joy to make this book complete.